Praise for *Missin*

Martha Birkett Bordwell describes a family's experiences of loss, motherhood, and international adoption in her memoir Missing Mothers. *Despite the complexities of modern life, this story is woven together as beautifully as a Guatemalan fabric.*

—Jim Johnson, author of
Text For Our Nomadic Future

By framing her memoir around missing mothers, author Martha Bordwell raises the ethical dilemmas and emotional consequences trans-national adoption has on families. Missing Mothers *addresses a challenging and necessary subject in accessible and intimate prose, inviting readers on a complex parenting journey. Through compelling considerations of race, grief and privilege, we uncover a deep empathy for people in families acting to transform loss and the unknown into acceptance, understanding and love.*

—Patricia Cumbie, author of
The Shape of a Hundred Hips

Much appreciation is due to Martha Bordwell for sharing her life story with the reading public. This series of vignettes flow through time and draw from the central theme of motherhood. Bordwell tenderly takes readers to the hearts of motherless daughters and mothers who give up children to adoption. They stretch to include women who struggle with their identity as good enough mothers. Bordwell's life was forever altered by the death of her own mother when she was six, and her feelings of grief and confusion in addition to her challenging relationship with her step-mother persist as she adopts a son and daughter of her own. Bordwell's honesty about this aspect of her life is the strength of this book and will sound true to any woman who has faced similar life events.

—Ann Murphy O'Fallon, author of
*Kiss Me Goodnight: Stories and Poems By Women
Who Were Girls When Their Mothers Died*

In her striking memoir, author Martha Birkett Bordwell takes her readers back in time to the tragic loss of her mother at a tender age where she learns to navigate life without her most essential caregiver. As she grows up with a loving father and a stepmother with whom she remains emotionally distant, Martha decides she would like to become a mother herself, hoping to recreate the connection she once lost. Through her painful experience with infertility and her bittersweet adoption of two amazing children, Martha bridges the many ways in which she and her family have been profoundly impacted by missing mothers. For anyone who has experienced heartbreaking loss, which will ultimately be all of us, this beautifully written memoir offers the promise of healing and a message of hope.

—Christine Friberg, Founder: She Climbs Mountains_
Creating Community for Motherless Daughters

MISSING
MOTHERS

a memoir

Martha Birkett Bordwell

Crooked Lake
Press

Copyright © 2019 by Martha Birkett Bordwell

ISBN: 978-1-7335353-0-4

Cover Photo: John Bordwell
Cover Designer: EBook Launch
Book Designer: Patti Frazee

Disclaimer

Missing Mothers is a work of creative nonfiction. Some names and identifying details have been changed to protect privacy. I have relied on my memory and on the memory of others to recreate scenes and dialogue, always endeavoring to present my story as truthfully as possible.

Missing Mothers is dedicated to the memory of
my father, Richard Birkett,

and to my children, Lucas and Clara, whose presence
is a constant reminder of my good fortune.

Table of Contents

June 2, 1950

Dear Nancy,

Just a note to enclose our
contribution towards the silver
for Bill. It will simplify matters
for us to have you get it.

We're kind of in a rush around
here tonite - getting ready to take
off for Mpls in the a.m. My
sister Marjorie is graduating
from Hamline U. Monday &
Martha & I may stay over for
that, - Dick has to be back
to work Mon. We're also going
to stop & see my folks tomorrow.
They haven't seen Martha since
last Aug. - isn't that awful?

Will see you at the wedding.
Since you're taking a couple

Prologue

The Letters

2009

Not even stopping to remove my coat, I rush into the living room and sink into a chair near the wide picture window. Removing the first letter from its envelope, I start to read hungrily, like a starving pauper. I open the next envelope, then another. I smile. I cry. Once or twice I stop to wipe my eyes. But immediately I start reading again, unable to squelch this impulse to imbibe every drop of what these letters hold. I don't stop reading until I have read every last word.

A few minutes earlier I had arrived home from work and was surprised to discover in my mailbox a manila envelope from Cleveland, from my Aunt Nancy. When I tore it open, out fell approximately twenty yellowed envelopes. A note in Nancy's neat handwriting was attached on top.

> Martha, your cousin Carol found these when she was helping me clean out my attic. When I first moved to Cleveland, your mother and I used to

exchange letters quite often. Jean wrote these between 1949 and '53. I wonder if you would be interested in them? I put them in order for you. Love, Aunt Nancy.

When I was six years old, my mother died. It was as if she walked out the door, locking it behind her, taking with her the key. Now, the door locked so long ago appears to have cracked open. My mother has reentered the room.

"Now the fun begins." starts the first line of the earliest letter, written in 1949, about a week after I turned one-year-old. It appears to be a thank-you letter to Nancy for a birthday gift. The letter goes on to say that I have just awoken from a nap and that Mother probably won't be able to continue writing. She implies that I am a bit of a handful.

Me! The responsible oldest child and only daughter? It strikes me that these letters not only paint a portrait of my mother but also of me, the little girl who likely spent more time with her mother than anyone else did in the years right before she died. The little girl who has never heard herself described in her mother's voice. That little girl is the central figure in every letter, at least until her brother is born.

And what do I learn about this little girl?

That she loved to dress up in the finery her aunt sent every birthday, to carry a blue purse, to pose for photos in her new green jumper.

That she won't walk outside when presented with her first snowfall, afraid to get her shoes dirty. She insists her mother carry her.

That a favorite pastime is standing on a stool in front of a window, watching for the neighbor's dog. Her papa made the stool.

That she likes the pull toy Nancy sent, but that Papa fixed it so it wouldn't keep getting tangled up.

That, at age four, she can't carry a tune, despite her musical mother's best efforts to teach her.

That her parents sometimes leave her with a babysitter named Mrs. Miller when they go to Papa's family farm in Wisconsin or to a football game in Chicago with their college friends.

That she quickly grows bored with her new baby brother.

That Papa is "still partial to Martha" after brother Tommy arrives.

And what do I learn about my mother?

That she likes to talk about clothes. That she goes "all out" on an Easter outfit after Tommy is born.

That she boasts good-naturedly about having her way with her husband, talking him into buying a new rug and painting the living room, insisting that she is going to drive the new car.

That she exchanges gossip about the love lives of his four unmarried brothers.

That she fishes for details of Nancy's love life.

That she has a Singer Featherweight Portable sewing machine and recommends this brand to Nancy.

That Nancy sent her a monogrammed thimble for her birthday. "When I saw that blue box, I couldn't imagine what I could be getting from Tiffany's," she writes. "It was a very thoughtful gift. I have already used it. Martha thinks that the thimble should be hers."

Most of her writing centers upon her children.

She chronicles our modest achievements: "Everyday she does something new." "She isn't as much work as formerly because she eats what we do. She won't let me feed her anymore, wants to hold her own spoon." "Martha says quite a few words now." "Tommy pulls himself up." "Tommy gets cuter everyday."

She sees herself as the central figure in our lives. "I'm the only one who understands her tho," she says of my budding vocabulary.

About Tommy she says, "Nobody holds him much because he spits up all of the time. Except his mommy."

She worries about Tommy's thumb-sucking and about my starting school when I am only four, since I have an October birthday.

She goes to a school meeting to learn how to prepare children for kindergarten.

She often refers to me as "Martha Ellen."

Regarding motherhood, she thinks "the first year is the hardest."

After Tommy is born, she writes, "I can't believe I have two children to my name."

These are mundane discoveries. No family secrets are divulged, no buried scandals. Yet to me they are golden because these letters tell the story of how my mother became a mother. And it is fitting that she is telling this story to Nancy, who is six years younger and not yet married. Will Nancy recall Jean's words when she is entrusted with mothering Jean's baby boy?

I read the letters again, more slowly the second time. More soberly. My image of my mother has been vastly altered. I have always viewed her as a tragic figure, a mother who died young, whose children either never knew her or can't remember her. But these letters reveal that her life is unfolding according to plan. It will be her family and friends who suffer a catastrophe when she dies suddenly.

On this March evening, I finally stop reading. I turn my gaze to the window and stare at the familiar trees lined up like sentries across our back yard, surrounded by crusty piles of late-winter snow. I listen to the rustle of wind spreading through the branches, highway noise in the distance as commuters return home from work. Behind the trees lies Crooked Lake, spreading outward like a cloak. I have lived on this Minnesota lake with my husband and children for over thirty years. I am temporarily living alone while John volunteers as a physician at a refugee camp in Rwanda. My children are grown.

A familiar feeling washes over me, as if rising up from beneath the quiet waters—a feeling of sorrow so great its strength weakens me, sinking my shoulders with heaviness. The letters aren't enough to assuage this grief. But they are a precious gift.

I run my hands over the smudged stationery, embossed with pink and gray flowers and feathers. I stare at the elegant handwriting that gently tilts rightward. I press my nose against an oily stain. I lift the stack and carefully put it back in the manila envelope. Then I place this unexpected gift against my chest, this envelope which contains long-lost memories of me and my mother, when I was a little girl and she was still alive.

Martha, Mother, and Tommy, winter 1954

1

Winter

February 25, 1955

Two days before her thirty-fourth birthday, my mother goes to the hospital to give birth to a baby, not to die. She does both, dying suddenly during labor, a lurking embolism entering her bloodstream and stopping her breath in its tracks. The gift she leaves behind, my baby brother, will cost her her life.

"Dick," she cries out to my father before she collapses, as the nurses rush to wheel her to the delivery room. The distraught doctor emerges minutes later to tell my bewildered father that she has died, but that he has saved my infant brother. He insists he has never lost a woman in childbirth before.

My own life will seem to begin this day, accompanied by a patchwork of moth-eaten memories forever etched in my consciousness. Recollections from before will soon lay buried, as memories of my mother sink into the shadows.

***

I awake early that February morning; the sky is still black. We are living in Carbondale, Illinois, where Papa had been transferred a few years earlier. I remember that Mother had gone to the hospital the night before, and that before leaving, she said something mysterious to my father: *My water has broken.* These will be the only words I ever recall spoken from her lips.

I scramble out of bed, my feet landing on the icy wood floor, sending bursts of cold up my legs. Seeking warmth, I rush toward my parents' room. Glancing into the living room, I am puzzled to see our next door neighbor Dorothy with a man I don't recognize, but later learn is Papa's boss. They are sitting across from one another, as still as stones.

The door to my parents' bedroom is closed. I push it open. Entering the bedroom I freeze, because from the bed comes a high-pitched whine followed by quick gasps.

"Come over here, Martha," Papa says. He pulls me into the bed, gripping me so tight against his chest I struggle to breathe. I can't see his face, but feel his rough and wet skin permeate my pajamas. He tells me, in ragged bursts, that my mother has died. I am more frightened of Papa's raw emotion than I am of his words, which will take time to sink in.

When my three-year-old brother comes into the room minutes later, I crawl out of bed and usher him away. "What's the matter with Papa?" Tommy asks.

"We have to leave Papa alone," I say, sounding more authoritative than I feel.

"Mama died."

***

Later that day, neighbors and church members file into our home, filling it with tear-stained and solemn faces, with quiet murmurs intermixed with sobs, with clanging silverware and tinkling cups, as the stunned women make coffee, serving the onslaught of visitors.

I crawl behind a couch, my legs rubbing against the

rough carpet. From my hiding place, I can hear my father's voice, high-pitched and halting, as he makes calls to relatives in Minnesota and Wisconsin while seated at a small mahogany desk.

A shadow darkens the entrance to my retreat. A strange woman reaches her hand toward me, encouraging me to leave my refuge. Reluctantly I comply.

That night we visit the funeral home in Carbondale, where my mother's body, clad in her best lavender wool suit, lies in repose. Papa hoists both Tommy and me in his arms to view the open casket, encouraging us to touch our mother as a gesture of good-bye. Instead I scream and turn my head away, while Tommy keeps pleading, "Why won't Mama wake up?"

Two days later, we travel by train from Carbondale to her home town in Red Wing, Minnesota, for the funeral. An executive with the Illinois Central Railroad, where Papa is employed as a civil engineer, meets us in Chicago and personally oversees the transfer of the body to the connecting train, an act of respect which must have meant a lot to my father. The new train stops in Milwaukee and my mother's Aunt Bertha boards. Mother had lived with this aunt while going to college. While Papa and Bertha confer quietly, Tommy and I run wildly up and down the aisles. The conductor comes and settles us down.

Tommy and I don't go to the funeral, instead cared for by one of my mother's cousins. Afterward, Aunt Nancy, my father's only sister, gets together with the other women in the family—which includes my mother's two sisters and her mother—to make a plan. Nancy seems in the best position to take the baby, despite having an infant of her own. In the fifties, it must have been assumed that a man would be incapable of caring for a baby by himself.

Dad will one day tell me about Nancy's offer: "I'll take David back home with me for a year, if you want. But I can't keep him longer. It wouldn't be fair to my husband, and besides, both the baby and I will get too close. A year will give you time to straighten things out."

When we return to Carbondale, Papa, Nancy, and baby David, who had stayed in the hospital while we went to the funeral, drive on to Nancy's home in Cleveland, leaving Tommy and me with neighbors. The next day Papa begins the almost six-hundred-mile trek back to Carbondale.

I imagine him leaning his car into the early March wind, snaking along two-lane highways. The ditches are bereft of flowers, lined instead with ribbons of gray snow. Perhaps he welcomes this solitary time, alone with memories of my mother. Maybe he uses these hours to construct a plan for a new future. But with Nancy's feminine voice and the baby's weak cry replaced by the monotonous drone of the engine and the harsh friction of wheels against pavement, he must feel himself totally severed from the rest of humanity. The road ahead holds little promise. At its end he will be faced with two frightened children and a house whose every pore will reek of buried dreams.

In Carbondale, Tommy and I are waiting, already put to bed. I toss and turn restlessly, jumpily aware of shadows shifting across the ceiling. Tommy is beside me, sticking to me like a magnet.

The doorbell rings. Our neighbor answers. I hear my father's voice, murmuring softly. "Sorry I'm so late. I thought about waiting until morning to get Martha and Tommy. But I was afraid they might be worried."

"Papa," I shout, running toward my father, grabbing onto his waist. Tommy follows. "Where's the baby?" I ask. I had been sure that Papa had gone off to find David. That's why he had been gone so long.

"The baby's going to live with Aunt Nancy. But you and Tommy will stay with me."

"Where's Mama?" Tommy cries. He begins to shriek. "I want Mama!"

2

The Halloween Surprise

October 31, 1977

Sitting in my work cubicle, I reach for the ringing telephone. "Your baby is coming tomorrow!" says the female voice on the other end. "I just got a call from Seoul. He'll arrive at 1:30!" She rattles on, most of what she is saying unheard.

"That's great!" I stammer. "I better let John know." My husband and I are expecting our four-month-old adoptive son, of course, but not until around Thanksgiving. I put down the phone, uncertain of what to do next. Should I call John? Make an announcement to my coworkers? Get in my car and start driving to parts unknown?

I rise from my desk and make my way toward the restroom around the corner. Entering the room, I lock the door and turn toward my reflection in the mirror. I press my palms on the counter, steadying myself, and look beseechingly at the face staring back at me—the wide open eyes, the permed red hair, the freckled skin which is beginning to redden.

"Do you know what you're doing?" I ask the young woman facing me. "Are you ready to become a mother?"

This Halloween promises to scare me like no other.

Returning from the bathroom to my cubicle, slinking into my chair, I call John.

"Can you get Dr. Bordwell for me?" I ask the receptionist, my voice a whisper.

"He's with a patient. Is it important?"

"Just tell him he's about to be a father."

"I'll go get him!"

"Martha, what's going on?" John sounds out of breath, as if he has been running, out of character for my unflappable husband. In my mind I picture his boyishly round face, the long-lashed blue eyes, the smile hidden behind a full beard, the white coat, the stethoscope hanging from his neck.

My words spew rapidly. "Lucas is coming tomorrow afternoon! The social worker just called. I'm getting ready to leave work. I can hardly think straight."

"Wow! I don't know what to say." He pauses. "Well, it will take me some time to get things in order here. I'll meet you at home later."

The rest of the day is a blur. I get colleagues to take over my responsibilities as an administrator of special education programs within our local school district. I arrange with my boss to start my maternity leave one month early. I make quick phone calls to friends and relatives. I race to Target to buy diapers and whatever else I think we might need.

But when I finally turn into our driveway at our home on Crooked Lake, where we have lived for just a year, I stay in the car, momentarily immobile. I stare at the newly barren trees lined up along the edge of our wooded lot.

Buttoning my coat and then opening the car door, I wander around the outside of the house toward the lake, my feet kicking away the dried leaves—their kaleidoscope of yellows, oranges, and reds blanketing the ground. I reach the lake and stare at its expanse of gray water, barely shimmering, two ducks gliding near the shore. I am remembering late October of one year ago, when I had been sure I was pregnant.

***

I awakened alone that Sunday morning, John having left for the hospital. As was my new ritual, I reached for the thermometer on the bed stand and stuck it between my lips. For two years I had been trying to get pregnant. Finally, success! My period was two weeks late. Monday I had a doctor's appointment. Unable to limit my excitement to just myself and John, I had confided the good news to my friend Sally the day before.

I removed the thermometer. I blinked. My temp was down. I shoved it back in my mouth. *I didn't leave it in long enough*, I insisted even as I reached between my legs and felt the familiar stickiness. I looked at my fingers, coated with red. My gut started to cramp.

I turned toward the window, curled into a ball and began to sob. After a while, I heard a scratching sound. I opened my eyes and saw the Norwegian pine which John had planted, its needles scraping against the first floor window. Its drooping shape reminded me of a solicitious old woman, a shawl covering her head, her shoulders sloped. I scowled at the old woman for the longest time.

"I don't think this is fair," I said out loud. "Don't you think this is ridiculous? First my mother dies in childbirth. Then I can't get pregnant. Shouldn't this be happening to someone else?" The old woman seemed to nod.

I jumped out of bed, stomped into the kitchen. I called Sally.

"I'll be right over," she said.

I began recklessly pulling flour, shortening, and sugar out of cabinets. When Sally arrived, she hugged me. "I wish I knew what to say to make you feel better," she said.

I nodded. We began slicing apples and throwing them into a pie tin.

"Pie therapy." We joked later as we helped ourselves to a second piece of the freshly baked pie. It never fails.

Sally left and John came home. He held me in his arms while I cried, both of us wondering if my tears would ever stop.

The next day I called the adoption department at Children's Home Society of Minnesota.

***

On Halloween night, as we greet neighborhood trick-or-treaters, John and I are the ones announcing a special treat.

"Our son is coming tomorrow, a month early!" I say as I drop apples and candy bars into plastic baskets shaped like pumpkins. Terror continues to surge through my body. On my face I have pasted a maniacal smile. John's smile is equally broad, but his excitement is apparently less complicated than mine. I wish I could steal some of his confidence.

After the trick-or-treaters stop coming, we lock the front door and get ready for bed. When John falls asleep, I am again alone with my thoughts and with my swirling cauldron of emotions. I am about to become a mother! At the moment I feel like an imposter, merely playacting my readiness to don the costumes of parenthood. As I again ask myself if I am capable of taking on this role, if I will do a good job, the answer seems painfully obvious. I feel an overpowering urge to swim away from these roiling waters. But it is too late.

There is nothing abstract about giving birth, I have read. But for me, who is not about to give birth in the physical sense, this night is eerily abstract. When I run my hand over my flat belly, I feel no bump, no movement, no baby's impatient kicks. When I caress my breasts, they too lay flat and unengorged. I feel no rupture, no water breaking, no oozing between my legs. When I turn over, I do so quickly, unencumbered by the heavy weight of an incipient life. I feel no sluicing of pain.

My child at this moment does not exist, just as my mother does not exist, not present to tell me my own birth story. I am not becoming a mother the way my own mother had. There will be no magical recreation of her birth experience with a happier ending, as I had once hoped. Instead, I am alone and about to become a strange baby's second mother, a role I never wanted. I wanted to be first.

My water has broken. These were the last, mysterious words I heard my mother say, words signifying the onset of her labor, signifying that my brother was beginning his birth journey from water to land. But the accompanying convulsions would unleash a murderous embolism into her bloodstream. Birth and death would be forever entwined.

I continue to knead my belly, willing myself to feel new life instead of loss.

*Martha, David, Dad, and Tommy at the farm where
Dad grew up, July 1955*

3

Motherless

March 1955

Two weeks after my mother's death, I stand on our porch stoop, wearing the brown tweed coat she had sewn, the coat with fancy epaulets on the shoulders. Underneath my dress I wear corduroy slacks to protect me from the March wind. I have been pushed out the door by Mrs. Hagler, the housekeeper Papa hired following Mother's death. She had been recommended by Mrs. McGowan, the obstetrician's wife, who phoned him two days after he arrived home from Cleveland.

***

"What are you going to do about a babysitter?" Mrs. McGowan asked.

"I'm not sure. Our next door neighbor might be able to help out."

"I have someone in mind. She's a widow who just needs

you to pay her Social Security contribution so she can qualify." Not having any other options, Papa quickly agreed.

***

As with other recollections, my memories of this first day back at school are riddled with holes. But a few memories stand out.

"They are all waiting to see you at school. Your principal will meet you at the door," Mrs. Hagler says.

"Do they know Mama died?" I ask. I don't want to be the one to tell them. Or to explain why we have no baby at home—the baby I had boasted about to my friends, telling them how my mother had said I would be her best helper.

"Everybody knows." Mrs. Hagler says. "I think your class has a present to give you."

Reluctantly I walk down the steps. I hadn't wanted to go back to school, crying and refusing to get dressed. So I am getting a late start. The other children are well ahead of me.

I wander down the sidewalk toward Springmore Elementary, shivering from the cold air. My legs feel heavy and slow. I examine each house, one by one. I walk by Mrs. Hanson's house. Papa says I am going to begin going there on Saturday afternoons to get my hair washed and curled. I don't want to go.

When I arrive at school, the principal is waiting. "We're glad to have you back, Martha," Mr. Knowlton says gruffly. His eyes seem watery. "I'll walk you to your class."

I blanch. I am a shy child, prone to hiding my face in my father's leg when meeting new people. But I am also afraid of Mr. Knowlton, whom I have never spoken to before. I reluctantly take his rough hand as we walk toward my first-grade classroom, the halls empty.

We arrive at the room, its imposing door shut, the leaded glass window shielding the activities on the other side. Mr.

Knowlton raps loudly. My teacher comes to the door, her face solemn.

"Welcome back, Martha." She begins to cry as she leans down to hug me, her clothes smelling of cigarette smoke. "Your mother was a wonderful person. I will miss having her as our room mother." I pull away. I have had more hugs in the last two weeks than I care to count.

"We have a present for you," Miss Adams says brightly. One of the girls comes forward with a wicker basket filled with yellow flowers.

I reach forward to take the bouquet. As with hugs, I have grown accustomed to being on the receiving end of one gift after another, my prize for having a dead mother. For the rest of the day it will adorn my desk, singling me out, shouting my specialness.

At recess all of the girls want to be near me, vying to hold my hand as we maneuver the playground. The boys hang back, except for one.

"Your mother is going to be eaten by bugs, did you know that?" Billy taunts. "I bet they are already climbing all over her face." One of the girls runs off to the get the teacher, and Billy is soon yanked from the playground. But it's too late.

At home that evening I approach Papa, who is sitting at Mother's writing desk going through a pile of papers. "Are bugs eating Mama, Papa?" I whine. "Why does she have to be put in the ground?"

Papa puts down his pen and pulls me onto his lap. "No, of course not," he says, his face turning blotchy. "Who told you that?"

"A boy at school. He got in trouble."

Papa shakes his head. "Mama isn't in the ground. She's in a beautiful box in Red Wing, in a nice room." It's true. She is lying in a crypt until the spring thaw, when she will be buried.

But that night I have a dream that I am stuck beneath snow, and rats are crawling all over me, nibbling on my face. I try to escape, pushing through underground passages. I can't find my way out. I jolt awake and my legs can't carry me fast enough toward my father's bed.

After that I refuse to sleep alone. Tommy joins me in Papa's bed. In the years to come I will never see my mother's face in my dreams. But when I have the dream about the snow and the rats, I will think of my mother when I jerk awake.

I have trouble sleeping, but my appetite is ravenous. My father will often tell the story of the time we went to his cousin Thelma's for dinner a few weeks after Mother's death, and I wouldn't stop eating mashed potatoes. "Thelma will think I never feed you," Papa protested, embarrassed by my gluttony.

When I am introduced to Thelma at a family reunion thirty years later, she cries, "You're the little girl who ate all of those mashed potatoes."

***

We get into a routine. Mrs. Hagler arrives every morning by taxi and leaves the same way every night after the dishes are done. She refuses to join us as we eat our dinner, claiming it wouldn't be proper. Instead, she sits by herself in the living room.

Sometimes Papa cries and won't stop. I go next door and get our neighbor Dorothy.

One day in early summer, after Mother has been dead for almost four months, Dorothy marches into our house, slamming the screen door. She has been helping us out on weekends.

"Jean is as dead as she is ever going to be," she says to Papa. "It's about time you start looking for someone to be a mother to your kids."

I am startled by the tone of her voice. Papa stares. His face reddens. His eyes start to blink, as they do when he is uncomfortable. Dorothy waits for her words to sink in.

"I have someone in mind. I know a woman who gets

her hair done where I do. She works at the toy counter at Woolworth's and has never been married. She said she would be willing to meet you."

Papa thinks it over for a week. Then my shopping-averse father takes us to Woolworth's.

"Can we really buy anything we want, Papa?" I ask. I can't believe my thrifty father is taking us shopping.

"One toy each."

While the friendly young woman at the counter helps Tommy and me choose, Papa looks her over, telling me years later, with a sheepish smile on his face, that he made note of her trim figure. I would guess this was a welcome sight to a man who hasn't embraced a woman in months.

She looks at me. "I bet you remember me. My name is Myra Mosby. I waited on your mother when she came in to buy things for the new baby. Your family is pretty easy to remember, with that carrot top of yours."

To Papa she says, "I heard about what happened to your wife. I couldn't believe it happened to such a nice person. I'm sure sorry about it." She demonstrates how the doll I point to can open and close her eyes.

Papa pays for the doll. As we walk away, Miss Mosby calls after us. "You take good care of your new baby, now." Carefully, I cradle my infant in my arms.

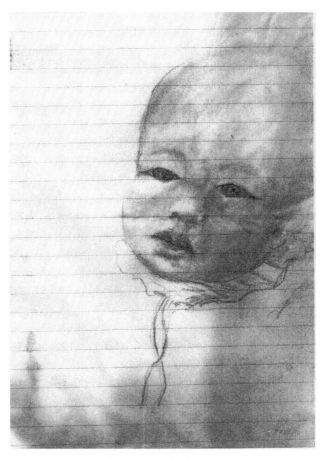

*Drawing of Lucas made during flight from
Seoul to Minneapolis*

4

Breaking Waters

November 1, 1977

Not wanting to upset him, and ashamed of my attitude, I haven't shared with my husband the depth of my anxiety about becoming a mother. As we drive toward the airport to meet our new son, I search the silvery late fall sky for signs of the baby who is steadily moving toward us. My mood is as gray as the clouds. Our child seems so far away at this moment, so unknowable. He is still an abstraction.

My baby has been packed up by his foster mother, anointed with her damp tears. Of course he has already emerged from his first mother's watery womb and travelled through her birth canal. Now he is in the midst of another transition. He is being separated from his birth culture. He is being divided into two beings: one Korean, named Byung; the other American, soon to be named Lucas.

As is our habit, we arrive early. We make our way down crowded corridors to the designated gate, where we are soon joined by other prospective parents, many accompanied by throngs of friends and family. I watch them intently as groups arrive, trying to discern their stories. Some seem to have birth children in tow, judging from family resemblances. Grayhaired grandparents are in abundance. Many hold balloons or handmade signs. Cameras in all shapes and sizes are being readied.

John and I are alone since we don't have family nearby. Even if some could have made it on such short notice, I don't think I would have welcomed their presence. Isn't that like inviting a crowd into the delivery room? Meeting our son for the first time seems a very sacred, private moment, even if it is taking place in a major airport. But if my mother were alive, would I want her here?

Yes.

We pace nervously. Suddenly the gate opens and a few people emerge. Chatter ceases as we all hold our collective breath. I hear our name called, the first announced. We raise our hands as everyone turns to stare. A young woman with long brown hair marches our way. "Your baby was the only boy on the plane," she says. "So we thought he should be first."

She places her bundle in my arms, while John snaps endless photos. And *voilà*, I am a mother. John and I are parents. Motherhood is less of an abstraction.

My anxiety is forgotten as I look at this baby with his shock of straight black hair, his smile as big as his oversized ears, his eyes little half moons because of his broad grin. He is dressed in traditional Korean clothing, wearing a shiny green jacket adorned with threads of gold. I can't stop staring at him, fascinated. I begin instinctively to rock him back and forth, the two of us rolling as one. I can't stop smiling. I can't stop crying.

"So you're Lucas," I say. "You're here." My baby smiles back.

And suddenly my lugubrious gloom seems utterly ridiculous. This child's smile suggests he couldn't be more thrilled to meet his new parents. He seems oblivious to the way his life is being upended with different kinds of faces to look at and different arms to hold him. His grin only widens.

After a few minutes I hand him to John. It is my turn to wield the camera. John's eyes sparkle with joy as he tenderly cradles his new son. "He looks pretty healthy," John says, as he too begins rocking back and forth. "I can't believe how alert he is after that trip."

An older woman, possibly the age my mother would have been, suddenly approaches us. Her hand thrusts forward a piece of paper.

"This is for you." She gives me a portrait of Lucas, a perfect likeness, drawn by pencil on lined notebook paper. "These babies are all so adorable, but he is my favorite." She is an ordinary passenger who has been transfixed by all of the Korean babies coming to Minnesota, but Lucas is the one she has chosen to draw. It seems a good omen.

I stare in amazement. "Thank you. It looks just like him. I will put the drawing in the baby book I've started." She smiles and wanders away.

We get ready to leave the airport, taking a last look around at the other families who are in various stages of picture taking, tears, and exclamations. Some are trying to calm their screaming children. Many of the older Korean girls, those old enough to walk off the plane, look dazed and exhausted. Interpreters kneel beside them, helping to make introductions and to explain. Briefly, my mood darkens. Their course is going to be much more difficult than our son's, I think, because of their memories of what has been left behind.

One of the girls— wearing a traditional Korean dress which dwarfs her tiny body and her straight black hair cut in a short bob—seems to be about six years old. She looks particularly bereft, holding her hands over her eyes and weeping, her shoulders heaving. When and how did she lose her first mother, I wonder? Has she grown up in an orphanage or in foster care? Or has she been separated from her family recently? Is she as frightened as I was at that age when I lost my mother? But I never had to cross an ocean, to leave my culture, to hear a foreign language, to lose my precious father. Silently I wish her and her family luck. I turn my gaze back to the face of my beaming son, who stares raptly at the bright lights illuminating the airport.

Strangely, we just walk away. We had arrived as two, now we are three.

We grow attached to our child in a matter of days, his needs quickly rising to the top of the heap. He sleeps through the night almost immediately, eats well, and greets everyone with a welcoming smile. But within a week he reaches back toward John or me when handed off to another. He is attaching too.

"This is way too easy," I say. It is hard to worry in the presence of such trust. But worrying is one of my strong suits. Two weeks after his arrival, I abruptly hand Lucas to John and say, "I'm going to bed." John stares at me, puzzled, but takes his child.

Climbing into our bed, I burrow beneath the blankets. My head peeks out just a little as I curl toward our west-facing windows. I seek the counsel of my confidant, the Norwegian pine, recalling our first conversation of barely a year ago.

"What's the matter, Martha?" the old woman seems to ask.

"I'm overwhelmed. It's too much responsibility."

***

Attachment is complicated, I am figuring out. My feelings for Lucas are unlike any I have ever had before, different from my feelings of love for John or other family. That this child is entirely dependent on us, that he could literally die if we neglected him, terrifies me. Suddenly danger lurks around every corner.

I begin to understand why the experts say that losing a child is the worst thing that can happen to a person. It is worse than losing a mother. I am also afraid of doing something to mar his perfection and of being unworthy of the trust apparently invested in me by his first mother.

I want to ask my mother whether she had ever felt unworthy of her children's love. I need her to bestow upon me confidence. To say to me, "You're doing a good job, Martha Ellen."

***

A little later John comes to bed. "What's the matter, Martha?" He echoes the old woman pine as he snuggles in close, his arms encircling my body.

"I think I'm having Postpartum Anxiety. Is that possible?"

"What are your symptoms?"

"I'm worried about Lucas."

"But he's doing so well."

"Yeah, but I don't know if we can keep that going. What if it's all downhill from here?"

"I think we're all doing great. Better than I had hoped." He rubs my shoulders.

"Things are going too well. It can't last," I counter. "What happens when he finds out that adopting was our second choice, not our first? He's going to feel bad about that."

"We'll cross that bridge when we come to it."

"But I feel so much responsibility. Not just to him, but even to his birth mother for putting her trust in us."

"We'll do fine." Soon John's rhythmic breathing signals he has gone to sleep.

I rise from our bed and move towards Lucas' room. I enter and stand beside his crib.

His breathing is as soft and even as his father's. I place my hand upon his.

A few days earlier, I had been functioning pretty well without this perfect child. Now John and I would be willing to swim across an ocean with our son on our backs if someone tried to take him from us. I can't imagine how we could survive without him. Still, I can't deny my sadness.

"I wish I was your first mother." I whisper. "I don't want to be second. I hate that you lost your first mother. Like I did."

I lean toward him, listening for the barely perceptible sound of his breathing. He is alive. My mother is dead.

I am reminded of the courage my father once summoned. How he told me, "I was devastated when Jean died. But I had to accept it. I had you and Tommy to think of. I was determined to keep you two with me and to bring David home."

Leaving Lucas to sleep, I wander back to bed. Suddenly chilled, I wrap myself in blankets and turn toward the window, where the moonlit Norwegian pine is waiting, her shrouded head bent toward the window as if she is straining to hear what I have to say now.

"My water has broken."

Martha, Dad, Myra, David, and Tommy, August 1955

5

Second Mother

August 13, 1955

Mrs. Hagler is holding the telephone, extending it toward me. "It's your father on the phone. He wants to talk with you." Puzzled, I lift the receiver to my ear.

Papa's voice sounds far away. His words are rushed. "Hello, Martha. Guess what? Myra and I got married today. Now we are going to Ohio to get David. We will be gone four days. Mrs. Hagler will take good care of you and Tommy."

"Should I tell Tommy?" I ask, twirling the phone cord in my fingers, not knowing what else to say.

"Sure. Go ahead. Tell him that you are going to have a new mother."

A new mother, I think. There's a silence. "Can I tell my friends?"

"Go right ahead. We'll be home soon."

I can't explain why Papa didn't tell us about this ahead of time or include Tommy and me in the wedding. Perhaps it had something to do with the fact that it happened so fast, two months after our trip to Woolworth's.

Tommy and I had gotten to know Myra before the marriage, of course. We were the wide-eyed little chaperones sitting in the back seat of the car on their dates.

A week after our foray to Woolworth's, Papa made an announcement. "We're going on a picnic to Crab Orchard Lake today. Miss Mosby is coming too." Papa has a boat out at the lake. We haven't been out there since Mother died, but in previous summers we were there every weekend.

I am relieved to see my father smiling again, having grown too accustomed to his frequent tears and his stricken face. And I love the lake. I decide not to mention that my stomach has been turning somersaults all morning.

Tommy and I climb into the front seat of the car for the short drive to Miss Mosby's house, where she still lives with her parents. She comes out carrying a picnic basket, wearing a white blouse tucked into form-fitting pedal pushers, showing off her slim waist. Her hair is a frizzy light brown, her eyes hidden behind glasses. I am impressed with how white and straight her teeth are, how full her lips.

We drive to the lake and begin walking toward the boat landing. But suddenly my stomach begins to cramp. I look down with horror at the greenish-yellow rivulets beginning to crawl down my bare legs. "I'm sick, Papa," I say.

My squeamish father turns green himself when he smells the stench. He stares at me helplessly. "We better get this little girl home," Miss Mosby announces.

Papa goes with Tommy to get the car while she rushes me into the ladies room and lifts me over the sink to wash off my legs. She takes off my soiled shorts, rinses them and wraps them in toilet paper. I creep ashamedly toward the car in just my underpants.

Papa drives home in record time. Miss Mosby continues

her take-charge approach, getting me into the bathtub, finding pajamas, offering me some Seven Up, putting me to bed.

I guess that is what you call baptism by fire. If this woman could handle this situation with such aplomb, she could raise three motherless children. Papa is sold.

***

Years later, Myra would tell me I took to her right away when she married Dad. My own memories are vague. I only remember being encouraged to call her *Mother*. And she insisted we begin calling our father *Daddy*.

Tommy's adjustment was a different story, she recalled. Neighbors told her that when they asked him how he liked his new mother, he replied, "You mean the lady who takes care of the baby?"

I wondered why Myra told me this, because it sounded so mean. But maybe Myra was used to hurt. She was the second of four daughters born to a woman whose husband's first wife had also died. In fact, Dad would one day tell me that his new father-in-law warned him, "You'll never find in your second marriage what you had in your first."

Myra's family was poor. She struggled in school. And to top it all off, all of her teeth were pulled when she was in her mid-twenties, due to widespread decay. She explained, "I almost had a nervous breakdown when I lost my teeth."

The first time I saw her without her dentures, her mouth collapsed like a pierced balloon, I recoiled in fear. She giggled, not with mirth, but with shame.

***

Normalcy was restored to our family when Dad married Myra. We became like our peers, with a mother who stayed home, expertly attending to housewifely duties, and a father who went to work every day. I was spared a revolving array of housekeepers or of becoming the woman of the house myself.

Having a stepmother was better than having no mother at all, wasn't it?

***

When I was ten, Myra gave birth to a healthy baby daughter. But when Lisa was just a few months old, I came home from school to find Myra, ashen-faced, talking frantically on the phone. Lisa lay in her crib. Why wasn't she moving? Why was she so pale? Dad arrived a few minutes later and they rushed Lisa to the hospital. She had had a seizure. The doctors didn't know why, but they put her on medication. I overheard Myra telling a neighbor that she might have to take it the rest of her life. Although the seizures eventually disappeared, with no obvious long-term consequences, Myra became a particularly over-protective mother to her youngest child.

Over time Lisa became more and more like Myra. She looked like her, with the same pert nose and compact body. Her voice began to sound like her mother's. She didn't like school.

I pulled away. I didn't want to be like Myra. We had different personalities. She was an extrovert, I an introvert. We had different tastes. Different talents. She loved to do crafts while I had two left thumbs. She had been humiliated by her teachers because she didn't learn quickly. I never saw her read a book. School, the academic side anyway, was my refuge. Once I learned how, I never stopped reading. I decided, on the basis of little evidence, that she didn't act like mothers are supposed to act. I pushed her aside.

I began pining for my mother in a way I hadn't at first. Jean was the woman I wanted to teach me how to be a woman. How to grow into a woman's body. How to be a mother.

AN AFTERNOON

If I could spend an afternoon with my mother, I would invite her to sit beside me on my living-room couch. I would study her face: its shape, the texture of her skin, the length of her nose, the shade of her eyes. Are her eyes as opalescent as they appear in photographs?

I would take hold of her hands, comparing their size to mine. Are her fingers long or short? Do her hands look as aged as mine do, with bas-relief veins spreading in all directions? I would look for the shortened life line on the left hand, the line which once worried me so, when it and its ominous meaning were pointed out.

I would compare our feet. Without anyone ever saying so, I have always been convinced that I got my nice feet from my mother. Unlike my wrinkled hands, my feet are pretty, as white and smooth as porcelain. They are just the right size, in my opinion, with no bunions or other protuberances. Surely my mother's feet would be pretty too?

I would ask her to stand beside me, comparing our

heights. Perhaps we would go somewhere and parade up and down, hoping to overhear someone say that surely we are mother and daughter, due to the width of our hips, the length of our legs or the rhythm of our stride.

I would listen to her voice, straining to hear my own within hers.

I would ask her to sing.

I would ask her to tell me stories, about her childhood, about her introduction to Dad, about her feelings regarding motherhood. What were her thoughts when she first held me in her arms?

"Do you have any advice?" I would ask. "Especially about daughters?" Because I'm about to become a mother to a little girl myself."

6

Expectations

January 1980

I'm expecting again. I'm expecting a daughter about whom
I know little. I only know that her mother told the nurses at
the hospital in Guatemala City that she was too poor to care
for another child. She already had a three-year-old daughter.
A social worker was summoned who carried the infant away
to an orphanage.

I know something else: She won't look like me. She
will be as dark as I am fair. No one will ever assume we are
mother and daughter because we look so much alike. And
that disappoints me.

***

Before we decided to adopt a daughter, I contacted a
local gynecologist, not quite ready to let go of my dream of
birthing a child. We had pursued infertility treatment with
him before Lucas' arrival.

"I would really like to give your husband a baby," said

Dr. Shadley, his eyes invisible behind his Coke bottle glasses. Shivering in an exam gown, my bottom chilled by the metal table, I wasn't in a position to argue. I nodded meekly, while the voice inside my head said, "Listen to yourself!" This was the same doctor who had once told my husband, "I'm sure the problem isn't with you." He apparently based this observation on the fullness of John's beard.

I asked "What would you recommend?"

"I'd try Clomid for a few more months. Or I could send you to the University."

***

Later, I told John about the appointment as we raked leaves in our back yard, Crooked Lake behind us. The acrid smell of burning leaves wafted from our neighbor's yard, coating my throat with a sour taste. Lucas was napping.

John shook his head. "I don't think it's going to work. I'm ready to adopt again."

I scowled at him, then stabbed the ground with my rake, sending the leaves skyward before they collapsed and fell. I felt a bleak solidarity with the trees shivering before me, their shed leaves carpeting the earth, littering it with blotches of red.

I glared. "I'm the one who gets insulted by these fertility doctors."

"Right, I don't want you to go through that anymore."

"I'm not ready to give up. They haven't really come up with a plausible reason why we're not getting pregnant."

John answered, "Medicine can't solve every problem."

I turned away, striking the leaves with more force. Neither of us said anything for a while. The sound of dried leaves being shoved into piles replaced our voices.

"I know how much this means to you." John moved closer. I turned away.

He backed up and began loading leaves onto a plastic

sheet, his movement slow and deliberate. He headed toward the garden, pulling the leaves which would be used to nourish next year's bounty.

I continued to rake, tasting the saltiness of my tears on my tongue, wiping my face with my sleeve. I stared gloomily at November's gray palette, the sky drained of color, the trees barren. I mourned the flame of October which had only recently departed.

When John returned, I said, "I just have always wanted to have a daughter who looked like you. With your pretty eyes. Or like me. Red hair." I paused. "Or like my mother. Or maybe have a child that sings like she did. Had her voice."

"Maybe we can request a baby who sings. Have a talent contest."

I smiled. "Maybe."

We stopped talking again as we concentrated on raking the leaves. Finally I said, "It will be better for Lucas."

"What?"

"To adopt."

"Probably. But he seems able to adjust to anything."

Our conversation stopped when I heard my little boy's voice. "Mommy, where are you? I woke up now."

***

I wanted to give birth to a baby because of my mother's death and my desire to bring her back to life, but I also gave up trying because of her death. I never felt afraid of dying in childbirth, although that might have changed had I become pregnant. But when you have a major loss early in life, you conclude that you are singled out for misfortune. You learn early on that life isn't fair. At the time, I wasn't that surprised that I couldn't get pregnant. In a way, I expected it. Infertility fit with my view of myself as unlucky and as being different from other women.

I told John I was ready to move on. But my misgivings

didn't go away. Could I be a good mother to a daughter? Didn't a woman need role models to be a normal woman and mother? And hadn't my experience with my stepmother taught me an unfortunate lesson—that non-biological mothers and daughters don't do so well?

And didn't my struggle with infertility suggest that I wasn't doing so great in the Department of Normal Womanhood, proving something about me, although I'm not sure what.

Who was I to take on the mothering of a little girl, especially a little girl who had another mother somewhere? Or would my own maternal loss be a blessing in disguise, creating a shared bond between me and my daughter?

Weaver near Antigua, Guatemala

7

Guatemala Threads

April 1980

On a rainy morning in early April, I hurry to the basement of our house on Crooked Lake to an out-of-the-way closet. Flipping the light switch, I survey the crowded space, searching for our battered largest suitcase. I quickly grab it from a back corner and lug it up the stairs toward Lucas' bedroom. I swing it onto his single bed. He has recently graduated to a "big boy's" bed, vacating his crib for his baby sister.

Laying the suitcase wide open, I begin to pack. Pampers. Undershirts. Onesies. Some of the clothes are used, having previously belonged to Lucas or other young relatives. Some are brand new. A few items are decidedly feminine: ruffled socks, pink tops and matching pants, a checkered dress covered with lace, little white shoes with rainbow colored ties.

"I think that should be enough for four days," I tell myself uncertainly. "And she probably already has some clothes." I raise an undershirt and scowl. Is it nice enough? Big enough?

Such foolish thoughts to be having at a time like this.

Sitting down on the bed, I gaze out the window, toward Crooked Lake. Through the bare trees on which buds have barely begun to form, I glimpse patches of pewter-hued water. The ice is breaking up. It should be gone by the time we return. Spring is advancing.

I try to shake off the anxiety I feel, so similar to how I once anticipated Lucas—and to will away my sorrow, because this isn't how I wanted to prepare to greet my daughter.

I wanted to give birth to her. I wanted to be there the moment she took her first breath, the moment she opened her eyes. I wanted to be the first image she saw, the first breath she smelled. I wanted to be the first being who sated her thirst, satisfied her hunger. I didn't want to be three thousand miles away on the day she was born, pursuing my ordinary schedule, oblivious to the fact that my future daughter had entered the world. I wanted to be able to tell her about her birth, maybe even visit the hospital where she was born one day.

And for my daughter's sake, I didn't want the first face she saw to be the face of a woman whose world had possibly been roiled by her conception. A face that resembled her own but that she would likely never see again.

The phone rings. I rise from the bed and rush into the kitchen to pick up the receiver. John is calling to tell me he has been able to book a flight to Guatemala City. We leave in two days. Unlike with Lucas, when our baby was delivered to us from Korea, we are required to go to Guatemala to claim our daughter.

"The third time's the charm," I say. Twice previously we were all set to fetch our six-month-old daughter. Both times we were told the paper work wasn't completely ready. But this time our social worker pronounced herself 100 percent certain.

While talking to John, my eyes focus on a colorful hand towel threaded through the refrigerator handle. When

I hang up the phone I grasp the towel in my hands and absentmindedly pull on its fringed borders as I recall the first time I saw it, in the shop where I was introduced to a mysterious country called *Guatemala*.

***

Three years earlier, in 1976, I was wandering along the banks of the Rum River in Anoka, Minnesota, where John and I had recently moved. I had plenty of time on my hands, as we had not yet conceived the baby we were trying to produce, and John was busy as a newly minted physician. Suddenly, I was intrigued to see a rough-hewn sign which said Native Arts of the Americas on a small building near the river's edge. I walked up to the door and pushed on it, unsure if I would find it open. But seated behind the counter was a pretty, petite young woman with a shy-but-friendly smile, long black hair, and fair skin flecked with cinnamon-colored freckles.

"Hola, I'm Teresa." Her speech was faintly accented.

I approached the counter. "I was just exploring the river. I had no idea you were here. You're pretty tucked away."

Teresa nodded. "We opened a few months ago. My husband's father owns the building. He grew up here."

"And where are you from?"

"Mexico City. I met my husband, Tom, when I was a foreign exchange student."

I turned around and began to survey the store's wares. "I love your clothes," I murmured as I sorted through a stack of blouses. "Are they from Mexico?"

"Mexico and Guatemala. We go there every winter on buying trips."

"I've been to Mexico, but I sure don't know much about Guatemala. I couldn't find it on a map."

"It's south of Mexico. It's very beautiful."

The brightly colored clothes, baskets, pottery, and wall hangings contrasted sharply with the natural wood of the shop's floors and walls. I learned that Tom had done the carpentry work.

While I purchased the decorative hand towel and a red and blue blouse, Teresa told me she offered lessons in Spanish, a language I had studied in high school for four years. I decided to register. Although working as a special education teacher, I needed more activities to occupy my time. I started visiting the shop on Saturdays.

A few months later, Teresa invited John and me to a Mexican-themed Christmas party held at the shop. At the party we faced a table bedecked with colorful tapestries, crammed high with Mexican delicacies. We met Tom—blond, long-haired and rangy—who towered over Teresa. He was as extroverted as Teresa seemed shy. The two, exactly our age and sharing many interests and opinions, became our first good friends in Anoka.

The following February, the two decided to try their hand at leading tour groups to Mexico. More than ready to escape a cold Minnesota winter, we enlisted. The trip opened our eyes to the artistic and culinary wonders of Mexico, whetting our appetites for similar travel. A year later we four travelled to Guatemala, accompanied by our new family member. Lucas attracted curious attention wherever he went, dressed up in little woven shirts and a straw hat collected along the way. He made friends with everyone with his crinkly smile.

We fell in love with the natural beauty of Guatemala as we traversed its hilly countryside. We visited Lake Atitlan, surrounded by slope-shouldered volcanoes and small villages, its turquoise water as clear as sapphire. On the dirt roads circling the lake, we bounced along in Tom's pick-up truck, watching groups of stocky women wading into the waters, their skirts rolled up. They bent low as they submerged their piles of laundry, then rose and wrung the wet clothing with muscular brown arms. Damp skirts and blouses dried on the adjacent rocks. Tom and Teresa told us these women were descended from the Mayan Indians, an ancient indigenous culture responsible for the magnificent ruins and mysterious stelae we would be exploring.

We visited the colonial town of Antigua. Three years earlier it had been devastated by a major earthquake. Huge piles of rubble lurked behind lovely blooms of bougainvillea.

One afternoon I made my way to Antigua's central square where long-haired women were kneeling, weaving at their backstrap looms, hoping to attract the attention of tourists. The brilliant sun illuminated their traditional loose-fitting rose and white blouses, featuring colors and patterns I would learn are symbolic of the natural world.

First I watched them from a distance. Then I approached a young woman with glistening hair through which ribbons were threaded. She perched on her knees, her hands in constant motion as she moved wooden slats up and down. Beside her were a pile of textiles for sale.

"Me gustan mucho." (I like these a lot).

"¿Cómo se llama?" I pointed to the blouse affixed to the woman's loom.

"Huipil" (wee-pil). Her smile was shy, revealing teeth rimmed in gold.

"A mí, parece muy difícil a hacer. ¿Cómo aprendió? (To me it seems very difficult to make. How did you learn?)

"Mi madre. Y mi abuela." She learned the technique from her mother and grandmother.

"Quiero comprar esto." I bought a used huipil, which is how they are often sold. It featured a brightly dyed green cotton; intricate rows of birds and flowers lined up across the bodice. The square neckline was embroidered with little five-petalled flowers in shades of pink, purple, red, and orange.

"Su bebé es preciosa," I said, leaning down to smile at the baby girl resting on her mother's back, drooping contentedly in a woven sling. "Muy hermosa."

It never crossed my mind that in a few years we would be welcoming our own Guatemalan baby girl.

∗∗∗

As I finish my packing for our trip to Guatemala, I hear John's car pull into the garage. He has retrieved Lucas from preschool. I stand at the top of the stairs as Lucas swings open the door and rushes forward. "Mommy!" he cries, flying into my arms.

"Did Daddy tell you the news?"

"We're going to fly on an airplane. We're going to find Clara!"

"Yes, we're going to find Clara. Clara Teresa."

NAMES

I am sitting on our summer porch, surrounded by weavings acquired on our trip to Guatemala with Tom and Teresa. Always fidgety, I twirl a strand of hair around a finger, reading a book while halfway listening to Garrison Keillor's *A Prairie Home Companion*. It is the summer we are waiting to receive a referral for the daughter we plan to adopt.

"I have a neighbor named Clara. She's an old Icelander." Bill Holm, a Minnesota humorist, begins in his deep and rhythmic baritone, simultaneously signaling wry amusement and seriousness.

I stop paying attention to his words at that point. My eyes drift to the lake peeking through the trees in our backyard on Crooked Lake and to the reflection of shards of light. In that moment Crooked Lake, and Mr. Holm, hand me my daughter's name. I whisper, "Clara," transfixed by its simple dignity, its tranquility, and its obvious meaning. Automatically I pronounce this name the way it is pronounced in Spanish, a sound that soars rather than sinks, like English vowels often do.

And not having consciously thought of it before, I remember that my mother's middle name was Clara, after her maternal grandmother, Clara Phelps.

"I have a name for the baby," I tell John later. "Clara, pronounced like they do in Spain and Mexico."

***

I don't know how my parents chose my name. Dad can't quite remember. I have to draw my own conclusions.

My parents were attracted to the old-fashioned English names of their ancestors. Ellen, my middle name, is a family name on my father's side. His mother was named Jessy Ellen and all of his siblings would give their first-born daughters her middle name. I am told my mother sometimes referred to me as Martha Ellen.

My mother's sisters were named Marion and Marjorie. I think Mother wanted to reuse the *Mar*. I think this because her sisters gave their first-born daughters the names Jeannie and Jane. Did they make a sisterly pact to give their daughters names that mimicked each other's? That's my theory and there is no one alive today to say otherwise.

My name is unfortunately associated with the wet-blanket Biblical Martha, the patron saint of housekeeping! Did that worry my mother? I like it anyway. I like its gravitas. I never wanted it reduced to a nickname. I didn't want to be among the sea of Lindas and Debbys and Kathys crowding the classrooms of the fifties and sixties.

I don't think my name sounds particularly melodius. But when I hear my name spoken, I hear my mother's voice. It is a good name for a girl whose mother died young, a girl who had to grow up quickly.

***

Naming one's child is one of the privileges of parenthood. But when one's child is adopted, especially from a different culture, the decision grows more fraught with uncertainty. If a family name is given, does that enhance the child's sense of belonging? Or does it eventually feel fraudulent to the child?

If a name consistent with the birth culture is given, does that feel alien to the parent? Or emphasize the child's differences?

And what if a child's name doesn't fit his or her face? What is that like for the child?

How does a parent know what kind of a child they are going to have, one who wants a name which blends in, or a name that stands out? Does the choice of name dictate who the child will become?

John and I were drawn, like our parents, to traditional names. Like our parents, we chose family names for Lucas' middle name. Stewart is John's mother's maiden name. Lucas Stewart: a name that connotes character.

Clara's middle name is Teresa, after our Hispanic best friend. Clara Teresa. It has a melodious lilt, like our musical daughter.

In my opinion, my children's names fit them well.

John, Clara, Martha, and Lucas at the orphanage

8

Clara Teresa

April 1980

"Q ueremos ir a este sitio." I explain to the Guatemalan taxi driver, handing him a scrap of paper with the address of our destination. We have arrived at the airport in Guatemala City.

"Sí, no hay problema." We climb in. Through his rear-view mirror the driver studies Lucas, his eyes curious.

"Una distancia larga?"

"No, veinte minutos, solamente."

"Gracias. He says only twenty minutes."

John and two-year-old Lucas look out the window, pointing to buses and trucks, while I stare at the slums on the hillside. I have read about the families who squat illegally on these scraps of land. Because we have travelled to Guatemala before, it has been easy for me to picture Clara's birth mother, who we have been told released Clara to a social worker at the hospital. I can imagine the shape of her body, the clothes she might wear, the hotel where she might work as a maid.

But I can't, or don't want to, envision where she might live. I shudder to think that our new daughter's birth mother survives as a squatter. How will I ever explain to my daughter that such crushing poverty led to her adoption?

We leave the congestion of the city. Eventually, our driver slows his car and begins weaving through what appears to be a residential neighborhood. He keeps checking the piece of paper, his head bobbing up and down. Finally, he pulls to a stop in front of a salmon-colored adobe house, its perimeter lined with calla lilies.

"Aquí está," he signals triumphantly.

"Gracias, Señor," I say as John whips out freshly changed Guatemalan bills and pays him.

"Is Clara here?" Lucas asks as we walk tentatively up to the door. I grasp his hand.

"I hope so," I say. "I think this is the right place." No signs identify the house as an orphanage.

John knocks on the door. A middle-aged woman, her round waist encircled by an apron, appears. "Buenas tardes. Estamos aquí porque nuestra hija vive aquí." I say, not exactly saying what I mean, limited by my Spanish vocabulary: "We are here because our daughter lives here."

"Bienvenidos!" the woman says, her smile broadening. "Vengan conmigo."

I tell John, "This must be the place."

We thread our way down a long hallway and then are introduced to another middle-aged woman moving out from behind a desk. She is dressed conservatively in western clothing, with big tinted glasses, and short, curly brown hair frames her face.

"Martha and John, welcome! I'm Mirna." Her English is good. She briefly grasps each of our hands. "And this must be Lucas." She bends town to take his hand. "Have you come to meet your sister?"

Suddenly shy, Lucas takes a step or two back, grabbing

my leg. I say, "It's so great to meet you, after corresponding all these weeks."

"This looks like a very nice place. We're impressed," John adds.

Mirna smiles. "We try to make a nice place for the children. Some of the older ones might grow up here. But I am guessing you want to meet Clara. I will go and get her."

While we wait, I gaze out the window at the lovely calla lilies leaning my way. I try to control my breath, as if I am in labor.

Suddenly a baby with a helmet of thick, black hair is being thrust into my arms. I stare at her bronze skin, her very round cheeks, and her enormous black eyes. Sturdy arms and legs poke through the lime green sunsuit she wears. Gently I begin to stroke her bare skin. I bury my nose in her hair, surprised to detect a musky odor, neither good nor bad, but distinct.

"Clara Teresa," I say softly. "Your mommy is here."

She stares up at me, as if taken aback. I immediately know that this child is going to be harder to win over than her brother had been. Her expression is more skeptical than trusting.

John remembers this scene differently. He recalls that before handing her to me, Mirna plays with her a little, rubbing her rotund tummy, making her laugh, showing us her likes and dislikes. Is she hesitant to part with one of her children, he wonders, or just doing her best to get the relationship started on the right foot?

"Would you like to see the orphanage?" Mirna asks.

"Of course. Can we take photos? We'll show them to Clara someday. I'm sure she will want to know where she lived for her first six months."

"Take as many photos as you like."

Taking turns carrying our wide-eyed daughter in our arms and holding Lucas by the hand, we are led through the small house. The wooden cribs in the room where Clara has slept are brightly painted. Child-friendly art decorates the walls. Toys are neatly lined on shelves.

In another room, older children are gathered at small tables having snacks and making crafts. They turn and stare, but don't run to us and cling, which suggests to me that they are getting their needs for affection met by the staff. They don't need to grab attention from strangers.

Lucas wanders toward them, curious about the snacks they are having. He is offered a cookie.

We return to Mirna's office. "You're free to go now. But can you come tomorrow and bring us back the sunsuit Clara is wearing? We will need it for the other children. And there is one more paper to sign."

I want to ask if I can keep the sunsuit. I want Clara to have something tangible from her time in this orphanage. But I don't want to be rude. "Sure. I have brought plenty of clothing for Clara with us."

We rise and walk out into the warm sun. John and Lucas hail a new taxi. I stare at my new daughter, who is eyeing me suspiciously. She turns around to look for Mirna, who has already disappeared behind closed doors.

Nestled in my arms as we drive back toward Guatemala City, Clara's demeanor is polite. She keeps eyeing me expectantly, as if to say, "Would you please tell me what is going on here?"

You tell me, I want to respond. This is strange for me, too.

9

Spring

April 1980

We check in at the Pan American Hotel, located in the center of the city. Huipils decorate the walls; staff in traditional clothing stand ready to serve. We eat a meal in the central dining room, then return to our simple room. The hotel has supplied a crib for Clara. Lucas squeezes in between John and me. Both children fall asleep quickly, as does John. I toss and turn.

We spend the next morning lying in the big bed in our hotel room, laughing as Lucas runs around the room or jumps up and down on the bed, entertaining his sister who chuckles audibly. Leave it to Lucas to break the ice. He doesn't seem jealous, possibly because, unlike with a biological child (before modern medicine allowed couples to know the sex of their unborn child), we have been able to tell him what to expect. He has seen photos. He has even been to Guatemala before. Even though he couldn't remember our trip, he could look at the pictures in a scrapbook. And airplanes and baby sisters and vacations had created a very positive connection in his mind.

Although she seldom cries, I immediately notice that Clara has episodes where she withdraws and stares briefly into space, oblivious to her surroundings. These "spells" will continue for weeks. I am convinced she is mourning the faces who are missing, her caretakers at the orphanage.

"Clara," I say gently, and her gaze returns to me.

We take our family on a brief tour of Guatemala City. In these days before inter-racial adoption in Guatemala rapidly expands, we see few other American families, none mixed race like ours. I have grown used to the stares of strangers since Lucas joined our family. But now the stares are even greater.

"Should we try Danny's Pancakes again?" John asks Lucas every morning.

"I want to eat the rabbit ones today," he announces with enthusiasm, referring to the shapes of pancakes offered. "Will the parrots still be there?"

"I think they live there."

"Why don't they have parrots where we live?"

"Parrots need warm weather."

"Why?" Lucas' questions never end.

As Lucas digs into his pancakes, six-month-old Clara's eyes grow as round as saucers when she stares at the colorful birds freely roaming the premises.

We wander back toward our hotel, stopping at various street markets. I buy Clara Guatemalan clothing, woven with the ubiquitous little animals and birds. I find an adorable purplish sunsuit and a brown jumper. I buy a bolt of multicolored fabric with the ambitious idea of making curtains for Clara's room.

***

We go back to the orphanage. "How is everything going?" Mirna asks, her voice kind.

"Great. Lucas is her favorite. But I think she is missing the people here." I don't mention the spells that have already begun.

Mirna lowers her eyes. "I will miss her, too. I get attached..." Her voice trails off.

I present several outfits I have bought on our shopping spree in the city's markets. "I hope these are appropriate for children at the orphanage?" I ask.

"Thank you. As you can quess, we really need clothes for the children."

"I wonder if we could keep the grccn sunsuit?"

Mirna hesitates. "When I see it, I will think of your daughter. Or of the other children who have worn it. I never forget a child who has lived here."

"Then you should keep it."

***

When the plane we board to return to Minnesota takes off, Clara for the first time begins to wail. "It's the air pressure," John says confidently. "Give her the pacifier so she will swallow."

"I'm not so sure. Maybe she is registering a protest at being separated from Guatemala. And from Mirna." *Are we doing the right thing*, I ask myself.

"You're overthinking. She'll stop crying when we reach a higher altitude."

We are taking her to the lake where she will grow up, surrounded by woods and wild life. From our Minnesota windows she will see pheasants and blue herons instead of parrots and emerald-hued quetzals, the Guatemalan national bird.

Arriving home, we are greeted by a note under the front door. I bend down to retrieve it. It is from a best friend.

Clara, welcome to Crooked Lake. The ice went off the lake today, a sure sign that spring has arrived. Thanks for bringing it with you.

I will soon put Steve's note in Clara's baby book.

When shown her crib, in the room she will share with Lucas, Clara stares apprehensively and clings to John. But when we turn on the musical mobile which hangs over her bed, its ribbons featuring dangling animals, her legs and arms start to jerk expressively and her face crinkles into a broad smile.

And just as they had with Lucas, neighbors arrive bearing gifts. A good friend brings dinner. Showers are held. Tom and Teresa, now living in western Minnesota and expecting their own first child, drive four hours to meet Clara. When told the baby's middle name, Teresa claps her hands with excitement, while her eyes fill with tears.

***

Two weeks after she arrives, I carry my fussy baby into the living room and sink into the antique rocker which I inherited from my paternal grandmother. Slowly I begin to glide back and forth. The room is pitch black, the only light coming from the moon and from Clara's bright eyes. She ceases crying but stares at me with her familiar gravity, as if trying to figure something out. Is she wary, as I am, about this journey she and I are beginning together? I with my pale skin and freckles passed down by my Scandinavian and English ancestors, my long-limbed body stretched out like a taut ribbon. She with her chocolate brownness, Mayan ancestry, thick hair, more compact body, round as a little ball.

As Clara finally drifts off to sleep, I continue rocking. A longing for my own mother powerfully encircles me. Although in adulthood my religious beliefs have morphed toward agnosticism, I have never stopped imagining that my mother is somehow keeping a protective eye on me. I begin a conversation.

I whisper, "We named Clara after you, Mama. But we say it differently."

"Didn't Dick tell you I always hated that name?" my mother whispers back. "So old-fashioned."

"He did, but I had already chosen the name. Don't you like the way we pronounce it?"

"It's better," my mother admits.

"The ice went off the lake the day we brought Clara home from Guatemala." I had never heard the phrase before I moved to Minnesota.

"A sure sign of spring," my mother answers.

"It's a good sign for a new baby, isn't it?"

"Perfect. New life."

My water has broken.

The ice went off the lake.

New life replacing what came before.

"I can't believe I have two children to my name."

"You're very lucky."

"Yes. But are our children lucky?"

"What do you mean?"

"Did they get the right parents?"

"There's no such thing."

My mother fades away into nothingness. But I am not alone. My daughter is still here. I tighten my arms around her, comforted by the movement of her breath.

My memory of this moment, rocking my daughter to sleep while longing for my own mother, will never fade. Clara won't remember, but I will.

MEMORY

I created baby books for each of my children. Each book begins with the letter and photos we received from the adoption agency, asking if we would accept this particular child as our own. The carefully dated scrapbooks are stuffed with documents and photos and my written commentary.

After the baby books were completed I added other scrapbooks, which today fill an entire bookshelf in our study. Inserted among the many photos are items such as birthday cards, school certificates, and occasional brochures related to a family vacation.

Here is what else I have saved: Every letter I have ever received. The clothing Lucas wore when he arrived from Korea. The dresses John's sister Lynda sewed for baby Clara. The sweaters John's grandmother knitted for our children. A quilt made by my maternal grandmother, given to me as a wedding gift. Children's books, pages torn, their backs broken: *Goodnight Moon, Frog and Toad Are Friends, George and Martha.*

Just in case anything happens, I want my children's lives to be documented. I want them to remember their childhoods. And I want them to know who I was and who John was.

I am sorry that they can't know who their birth family was and that a book can't be created telling that story. Their backstories are limited to one page in each of their baby books.

But my children don't seem particularly troubled by their unknown pasts, perhaps because they assume their mothers never spent much time with them after their births. There is nothing much to know.

***

My mother and I spent six years together. She made a baby book for me. It is meticulously maintained, starting with information about when she went into labor and when I was born. It describes my failure to gain weight, resulting in a switch from breast- to bottle-feeding. It notes when I took my first step and when I was toilet trained (thirteen months!). Difficulties getting me to go to sleep at night are mentioned. All of the illnesses I ever had are listed.

The final entry is written in Dad's handwriting. I had German measles in November 1954, three months before she died.

Of all my family, Dad did the best job of keeping my mother's memory alive. He talked to me about her, usually a bit furtively, when only I was around. He took us to Red Wing to family reunions. He kept her photo albums and gave them to me. Toward the end of his life, he wrote, in longhand, the story of their courtship, marriage, and her death, which I have relied on in telling this story. He made copies of photographs from family slides and gave each of his four children a set, telling us each, "Here is the story of your childhood, right here." I cherish it all.

Still, I wanted more. I wanted my mother's jewelry. I wanted the clothing she had sewn for me and my brother. I wanted to try on one of her dresses, to see if it fit. I wanted the books she had read and the records to which she had listened.

But these objects were mere substitutes for what I really wanted. I wanted my mother to be more than a shadow. I wanted to remember my mother. I wanted to have my own private memories, instead of making do with the recollections of other people. I wanted to remember her voice. I wanted to be able to say, when a song came on the radio, "I remember when Mother sang that song." Or to have my eyes fill with tears when a certain fragrance reminded me of her. I wanted to remember the feel of her body.

I am angry at myself for not remembering her because I spent more time with her than anyone else did in the years before she died. I shouldn't have forgotten. My clear memories begin the day of my mother's death, when I entered my parents' bedroom and found Dad crying.

When my mother died, it was as if she took my memories with her.

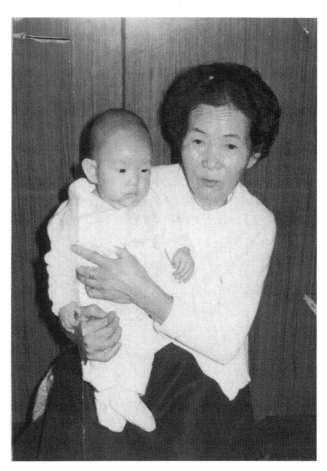

Lucas and his foster mother, 1977

10

And I'm Never Going
To See Her Again

November 1979

Lucas presses against me as we make ourselves comfortable on the couch. His hair smells of baby shampoo and his pajama-clad body feels soft. Beneath our feet lies our Brittany Spaniel, Reuben. John is seated in his recliner nearby, leaning forward, his eyes tender and engaged.

We are about to have "the talk."

"Let's look at your scrapbook, Lucas." I say, reaching for the ivory-colored album on the coffee table. Lucas takes the book from me and opens it. He knows the story pretty much by heart.

***

Barely two years previous Lucas had swooped into our world, as light as a feather, with only the shirt (and pants) on his back and the sparsest of backstories. It was as if his lack of a past lightened his load as he moved from one identity to another.

He immediately employed his considerable charms to ingratiate himself into every pore of our beings. Mainly it was his smile which won us over, the smile which caused his eyes to crinkle and disappear.

Our spirits soared as we heard Lucas' praises sung, with the implied message that we, his parents, deserved some of the credit. Babysitters told us what a gem he was. Friends marveled at his affability. We knew deep down we hadn't done much to deserve such accolades, but we basked in their glow anyway.

But there were also times when my fears about keeping my little boy safe seemed prescient. When he was two I poured scalding tea water on his nose. I was holding a tea cup and didn't realize until I heard his screams that I had tipped it slightly, spilling it on the little boy standing beneath me. The burn formed blisters and eventually a slight scar. I feared I had inflicted permanent damage, both physical and mental, on my perfect child. When John came home from work the next day, Lucas shouted cheerfully, "Mommy didn't burn me today, Daddy."

Lucas was resilient, easily bouncing back from the mistakes made by his novice mother. He forgave me when I found it hard to forgive myself. He gave me a priceless gift: confidence in myself as a mother.

Shared experiences accumulated. We repeated his first words and coaxed his first steps (immortalized with a photo). Every night we read books together: *Good Night Moon, Frog and Toad, The Berenstein Bears*. We celebrated his first birthday, which included his first taste of ice cream, which led to another first—learning to navigate a spoon to his lips. We took vacations to see grandparents in Iowa, friends in California. And, especially, we spent time together on Crooked Lake: frolicking in the water on summer afternoons, jumping in piles of leaves in the fall, planting seeds in the spring. That is how we developed a shared narrative about our family. These experiences became so much more important than a shared biology.

Nonetheless, Lucas' Korean ancestry needed to be brought to light. We couldn't be afraid to acknowledge it.

***

Drawing Lucas in close, I look down at the first page of the scrapbook. I begin to read the words I have written in longhand. "This is the picture that Children's Home Society sent to me and John. We looked at it and felt so happy because it meant Lucas was going to be our new baby boy."

Lucas scowls suspiciously at the grainy black and white photo of himself. It shows him leaning back into a reclining seat in which he has been placed, his skinny legs splayed, his facial expression dyspeptic. I had the same skeptical reaction when I first saw it. John and I had decided to take a leap of faith, disregarding this poor quality photo.

"But your name wasn't Lucas then, was it?"

"No, I had a Korea name."

John asks, "Do you remember what it was?"

Lucas shakes his head. "I forget."

"Byung Il Yoo."

"That's a silly name."

"It's a popular name in Korea." But I am not sure which is the first and which is the last name. Korean names confuse me.

"I'm Korean." he says, sounding proud. I'm pleased. We want him to be proud of his heritage.

"Yes, Korea is where you were born." John nods.

"And who is she?" I point to the two photos of an older woman holding Lucas. Neither is smiling, as both stare soberly at the camera.

"My foster mom?"

"Right! She took good care of you until you could come to Minnesota."

"She got me ready."

"Yes."

He turns the page. "What does this say?" He points to a smudged, type-written letter.

"It tells Mommy and Daddy all of the things they need to know about you. Like what you like to eat and when you like to sleep." I read what it says on the line labelled "Character": "He is a strong, lovely and affectionate child. He is not spoiled. He has a lovely smile." Does that sound like somebody we know?"

"Me!"

"Just like you!"

He turns the page. All of a sudden we three are at the airport. I hold Lucas in my arms. "And when everything was ready, your foster mother took you to the airport and you flew across the ocean to Minnesota, where Mommy and Daddy were waiting."

"I know. I saw the fish."

"You remember fish?"

"I looked out the window. I saw a whale."

He pretends the couch is an airplane, extending his arms like wings, making a buzzing sound. He leans over the armrest and looks down, pointing. "Look. A big whale. I saw birds too." He looks upward.

"It must have been exciting to fly in an airplane." John smiles. Lucas nods.

He turns the page. The drawing on lined notebook paper, given to us by the older passenger, stares back. "A lady made this," Lucas says.

"Yes, she chose you to draw because you were the only boy on the plane. And because of your smile."

"She's a good draw-er. It looks like me." We nod.

"And then we took you home to Crooked Lake." John and baby Lucas are posed for a photo on our living room couch.

"Was Reuben waiting?"

"He sure was. I think he was a little jealous."

"Were you jealous, Reuben?" Our Brittany Spaniel briefly raises his head, then goes back to sleep.

I steer the conversation in a different direction. "Lucas, do you know what the word adoption means?"

"I'm adopted."

John says. "That's right."

I say. "It means that you had another mother before you came to Minnesota."

"I grew in her tummy." We had had this conversation before.

"And then when you were born your first mother couldn't take care of you, so even though she loved you very much she decided to find a new home for you."

"Why couldn't she take care of me?"

"Korea is a very poor country so she didn't have enough food."

"Why is Korea poor?"

John says, "They have had a lot of wars."

"I don't like wars," Lucas says.

"No one likes wars," John says.

"So after the war everyone was poor and some mothers had to give their babies to other mothers to take care of them. I'm sure it made your mother sad to give you to your foster mom."

"And I'm never going to see her again." His voice is cheerful. Certain. Hopeful. I look at John. I was expecting a different attitude. Sadness. Curiosity. More questions.

John answers, "No."

Lucas closes the album and jumps off the couch. He retrieves a different book from a shelf. "I want to read this now." He hands me *Frog and Toad Are Friends*.

"Okay, we'll look at your scrapbook some more another time." He shoves it away.

***

A few weeks after our adoption conversation, Lucas is running feverishly around and around our free-standing fireplace. Reuben is trying to keep up with him, his four feet sliding haphazardly on the wood floor. Finally Lucas slows and runs headlong into John's lap.

John reaches out to pull him up into his recliner. Grizzled and grimy from a four-day hunting trip, he has just arrived home.

"I re-mem-ber you." Lucas, says, struggling to pronounce this three-syllable word.

John's expression turns serious. "Did you think I wasn't coming back?" he asks. Lucas doesn't answer. He burrows into John's arms. "I remember you too." John says. Father and son rock back and forth, clutching one another in silence.

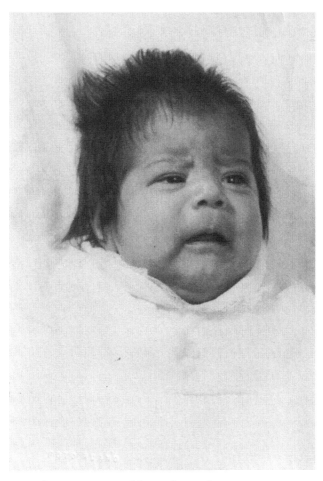

*Photo we received from the orphanage prior to
adopting Clara, 1979*

11

I'm Crying Because
You're Not There

September 1982

Three-year-old Clara holds her baby book on her lap, its cover decorated with pairs of jungle animals. Hippos relax in a stream, pelicans and flamingos sun themselves on the hippos' backs. Monkeys perch in trees. Studying this book is one of Clara's obsessions.

"I'm crying because you're not there, Mommy." she says solemnly, pointing to the first photo sent to us from the adoption agency, the grainy black-and-white image in which she looks perturbed.

Cleaning up the kitchen, I freeze, stunned by her choice of words. I am too dumbstruck to respond. What is my little girl trying to say? That I, not her birth mother, am the mother who once was missing?

Again, my child is educating me. Letting me know I have it all backward. That it is I she once missed, the mother she didn't meet until she was six months old, not the mother who gave her to a social worker at the hospital where she was born.

I realize that I, unlike my prescient daughter, have repressed regrets about those six months when she and I were not together. I have willed myself to forget the sadness I felt at not being with Clara during her birth, during her first few months and of having no memories to share. But I had never considered our shared loss from this perspective.

I walk into the dining room and pull Clara into my lap, tears running down my cheeks.

"I wish I had been there, Clara," I whisper. "I wish that so much." Clara holds on tight.

I recall a scene from a few days earlier. Clara put talcum powder all over her dark-skinned arms, proudly proclaiming that now she has white skin. Then she shyly asked, "When am I going to start looking more like you, Mommy?" Thrown off course by this comment, I blurt that she is so beautiful, I wish I looked like her.

"But when will my skin turn white?"

"Your skin isn't going to change color, Clara. But your skin is better than mine. You know how Mommy's skin is always turning red, getting burned."

She begins to cry, as if heartbroken. I haven't given the answer she sought. I once wanted her to look like me. Now my beautiful daughter wants the same. And neither of us can have what we want.

I imagine myself at Clara's age. I recall an old photo of myself wearing an oversized dress which pools around my feet. I also wear high heels. I am wearing my mother's clothes. By wearing her clothes, I am trying to become her.

Clara yearns to connect with me in every way that she can, physical appearance being the most obvious. When I was Clara's age, I must have loved my mother as much as Clara loves me.

Later, while my daughter naps, I pick up the scrapbook

lying on the floor and carry it to the couch. Propping it on my lap, I smile at the whimsical cover, at the sly eyes of each of the grinning animals. But when I open the book, I am confronted by the black-and-white photo, by the furrowed brow of my motherless daughter.

I read what I have written on the first page of the scrapbook. It begins, "On January 15, 1980, we received the call we had been waiting for." Clara would have been three months old at the time. What was happening in Clara's life while I wrote this passage? Who was holding her? Who was feeding her? Who was sheltering her?

I continue to turn the pages. I read that after we received the photo, we called to tell the agency we accepted this referral. I wrote that we showed Lucas the photo and explained to him that he was going to become a big brother. We told him we would fly in an airplane to get her. That prospect excited him as much as the prospect of a sister.

A few pages later I wrote a passage noting the name we chose for our daughter, listing the various layers of meaning. And a few pages after I reported that two times we prepared to fly to Guatemala, only to be told that the paperwork wasn't ready.

I wrote that on the morning we finally leave, we hear Garrison Keillor announce on his *A Prairie Home Companion* show that, "Martha, John, and Lucas are on their way to Guatemala to get their daughter Clara, who they are adopting." Garrison was in the habit of sending out personal messages requested by his listeners. He was supposed to play a marimba tune but never got around to it.

I keep turning. Each page is accompanied by photos: Lucas at the airport, excitedly pointing to the airplanes outside the window; Mary, our social worker, seeing us off.

And then comes the photo showing us at the orphanage holding Clara for the first time. Clara's head is turned toward me, her expression pensive. Mirna stands behind a yellow crib holding Lucas, who seems to be struggling to escape her arms.

The story of Clara's adjustment to life in Minnesota begins to unfold. I read the note from Steve, about the ice going off the lake, dated April 14, 1980. On the same page is a photo of him holding Clara. She is wearing a self-satisfied smile, developing a taste for being the center of attention. I see photos of baby showers, of meeting her grandparents, of Lucas' third birthday party. Ice cream drips down her chin. She is mugging for the camera, her eyes squinted shut, stealing the show.

Although Clara had a more serious side to her personality than Lucas did, in fact her adjustment was almost as easy as his. She slept and ate well. Her staring spells ended after a few weeks. She smiled more and more.

In the scrapbook, I have recorded the exact number of teeth she had acquired by August and her first word (Roo, after our Brittany Spaniel, Reuben.) A later page records her first step and even includes a picture of her taking it. (A reenactment, I would guess.)

I turn to the photo on the last page. Lying on a blanket in the front yard of our home at Crooked Lake, John smiles at the camera, his full beard hiding most of his face, except for his sparkly eyes. Lucas is running his way, about to jump into his arms. Clara, sitting beside John, also smiles at the camera—at me. Her arms are lifted as she moves them up and down rhythmically, her go-to gesture when feeling excited.

I reach for a pen, and beneath the photo I write, "I'm crying because you're not there."

I date it: September 10, 1982

12

Motherland: Red Wing

July 4, 1959

D ad turns sharply onto the gravel road leading into the Burnside Cemetery outside of Red Wing. He slows our station wagon to a crawl, inching toward the two century-old white oaks that mark our destination. He stops and yanks out the parking gear.

From my back-seat view, I see that his eyes are already starting to blink. His lips are quivering. As if it's contagious, I follow suit.

"I'll stay in the car with Lisa," Myra says, her arms encircling my baby sister.

"Come on, Davey," Dad says to my four-year-old brother, who jumps at the chance to escape the confines of the car. David is an energetic child with curly blond hair covering his head. He's smart as a whip, despite the fact that doctors feared he might be brain-damaged due to lack of oxygen during his birth.

Dad takes long loping steps toward the big headstone marked Sargent, holding David's hand. Tommy and I follow behind. I whimper while Tommy scowls suspiciously.

I see my mother's headstone:

Jean Sargent Birkett
February 27, 1921–February 25, 1955.

David at Mother's gravesite in Red Wing

"Here's where your mother is buried. Next to Grandpa Sargent," Dad blurts, wiping his eyes with his sleeve. He has recently told David about our mother's death. He must believe that David has understood better than he has, as David just stares, pulling his hand away from Dad's clutch. He immediately starts running in and around the headstones.

I hear Myra shout, "David, get back here." He runs to the car and Myra pulls him in, ordering him to settle down.

The three of us, Tommy, Dad, and I, stand with hands hanging awkwardly, all of us crying now. My tears slide down into my mouth as I reach out my tongue to catch them.

Tommy's eyes lurch from Dad to me. In the background I hear the din from the cars speeding by. Dad tries to muffle his sobs.

I try to get hold of myself by imagining what it would be like to reach down into the ground and pull out an alabaster bone or two, run off with them like a triumphant dog, hiding them where only I can find them. This thought scares me, because it seems like an entirely possible act. All I would need is a shovel, right? And to grow up, so I could drive myself here in the dark of night to commit the reasonable act of dislodging a relic of my mother. But somehow I know it's impermissible. (Years later, when my father dies and I actually am given his remains in an urn, I never open it, horrified that my father could be reduced to mere shards of bone and ash.)

Dad pulls me and Tommy toward him, his arms encircling us for a brief minute. None of us says anything. Letting us go, Dad turns around and starts telling Tommy and me about the other relatives buried nearby.

"This is your mother's Uncle Cecil, who married a woman named Cecil." He smiles a little at the absurdity. The two Cecils are buried side by side.

"And here are more of her uncles. They all died young. Heart disease." This particular family history unsettles me, forecasting future doom.

He turns back to my mother's grave. "Grandma Sargent will be buried here too, next to Grandpa and your mother, when she dies. Well, let's go," Dad says. We walk by the potted blood red geraniums. I turn for one last look. I want my mother to come with us. She is the one who can show us around and break the ice with the relatives we are about to join.

We climb back in the car. David bounces up and down. Lisa is dozing in Myra's arms. Myra, who also has tears streaking down her face, steals a quick glance toward Dad,

then again admonishes David to settle down. Dad turns the
car around and we drive away from my mother.

In the backseat of the car, eight-year-old Tommy
whispers, "Who is Jean Sargent?"

I stare open-mouthed. "You know!"

"No I don't. No one ever explains anything to me." His
voice sounds accusing.

"She's our mother. She died when David was born. I
know you know!"

At the time, I was sure Tommy was pretending not to
remember Jean. But I eventually understood that he wasn't.
Our family seldom talked about her. No photos of her graced
the mantel. No childhood recollections were recited over
dinner. In the fifties, stoicism reigned. It was considered best
to move on. Tommy was too young to recall our mother, or
the fact that she died. Too young to understand the reason for
her disappearance, he must have mainly experienced it on an
emotional level. And he must have been devastated. We all
suffered when Jean died, but I believe Tommy suffered the
most.

Sometimes I think that Tommy may have been Mother's
favorite child, just as I seemed to be Dad's.

***

My cousin Ann gave me a CD a few years ago containing
8 mm scenes her father recorded from the Sargent reunions,
which our family attended every year. One scene stands out. I
always cry when I watch it.

My towheaded brother Tommy, about two years old and
wearing a seersucker sunsuit and a determined expression, is
dragging a recalcitrant pull toy behind him. All of a sudden he
bends his head backward, his face taking on an expression of
such radiance I can't help but wonder what he sees above. His
arms raise skyward. Gradually my slender mother, wearing a
shirtwaist dress and an equally radiant smile, comes into view

as she leans over to pick him up. She hoists him up to her shoulder so that he is looking toward the camera. I have never seen Tommy smile like that.

Then Dad and I appear and our family of four walks away from the camera, my dad holding his hand on my mother's back, his other hand holding mine, Mother carrying Tommy. As if we are leaving the party, as if the movie is ending. I can almost hear the credits role.

Tommy seemed to stop smiling after our mother's death.

***

After leaving the cemetery, we approach our next destination, the Sargent Nursery, down the road on Highway 61. Lush hanging planters grace the perimeter of the entire nursery. Red, white, and blue flags are draped in between the planters. We park in the lot and gather our things: a picnic basket, folding chairs, Lisa's diaper bag. We head left toward the white Cape Cod house next door, where my mother's cousin Max, who runs the nursery, lives with his family.

We are here for this annual gathering of the descendants of my great grandfather, which included nine sons and a daughter. It is the one day of the year we remember Jean, although even at this reunion her name is seldom mentioned.

I always feel like an outsider at these gatherings. I sit beside my grandmother, trying to get to know her. Grandma Sargent, whose once-red hair reveals just wisps of orange, who is stout, a bit bent over. She has recently moved to an apartment in Red Wing following my grandfather's death. Grandma is very reserved, apparently taking after her father, a laconic immigrant who she tells me never talked about his childhood in Sweden. The only time she ever spoke to me about my mother, she said, wringing a handkerchief, her eyes focused on her lap, "I asked God why he didn't take me. I had finished raising my children."

"How pretty you are getting, Martha!" exclaims Aunt

Lois, my mother's brother's wife, who is wearing a red, white, and blue sundress. I am pleased by her words, though not entirely convinced. Marian and Marjorie, my mother's sisters, ask me about school. Marjorie, tall and slender, resembles my mother.

I wonder what it would be like to watch my mother interact with her sisters. Watch them banter like my father does with his brothers.

Of all my mother's siblings, I loved Aunt Marian the most. She was warm and non-judgmental, beautiful, with a luminous smile. When she is in her early sixties, she will be diagnosed with inoperable breast cancer. John and I will be living in Minneapolis by then, where she lives. I will visit her often in her final weeks, seeing myself as a sort of stand-in for my mother. I will ask her questions about Jean sometimes, but the answers she gives will be vague and unsatisfying.

I will ask her once, "What are you most afraid of about dying?"

"That I will be forgotten."

Was she remembering her sister when she said those words?

***

My mother was the second of five children, the oldest girl. Her father never showed much talent for making money, moving from job to job. According to Dad, the family's poverty was particularly hard on my mother, because many of their relatives were successful and prosperous. Jean was humiliated to receive her cousins' hand-me-downs.

Grandpa tried farming for a while, then had a business delivering eggs. When my mother was in high school, he bought a chicken farm.

When Mother graduated from high school, there was no money for her to follow her older brother to college. But she had another plan. In high school she was part of a singing trio whose friends told them they sounded as good as the Andrews Sisters, who also happened to be from Minnesota. After graduation the three friends moved to Minneapolis, got jobs as nannies during the day and sang in supper clubs at night. Her teetotalling, religious family was horrified by this career choice. Aunt Bertha came to the rescue, offering to lend Jean money to attend college. Jean moved to Milwaukee to go to business school, living with Bertha, sleeping in a Murphy bed in her aunt's one-bedroom apartment. Later she decided to follow in Bertha's footsteps and become a social worker. Bertha, probably flattered by this emulation, continued to invest in her niece's education after Jean moved to Madison to attend the University of Wisconsin. That is where she met Dad.

***

In the midst of the reunion, I notice my mother's younger cousin Carol watching me. Short, curly haired, and outgoing, she walks my way.

"Martha, I've been listening to you talk. It's so strange. Your voice sounds just like your mother's."

I stare, my face flushing, half with embarrassment, half with pleasure. All of a sudden I don't know what to say. It's as if Carol has broken a rule, bringing up my mother. "And you walk just like her, too."

"What do you mean?"

"Well. You know you and she are shaped quite a bit alike. I think you are going to be tall like your mother was. You have the same long legs."

She smiles kindly. The conversation ends, as someone else comes up to talk. But I have never forgotten her words. What would it be like to stand beside my mother and listen to others comment on our resemblance? Or to be able to gaze at my mother and infer how my barely pubescent body was going to turn out? To envision that aspect of my future?

Soon I see Carol and Dad engaged in a private conversation. I learn years later that she was encouraging Dad to write down his memories of our mother and the circumstances of her death for his children. He'll follow through one day and I will use his words in telling parts of this story.

***

After the reunion we drive through Red Wing's picturesque downtown, a tourist attraction because of its proximity to the Mississippi River.

We hike up to Red Wing's famous Barn Bluff, on the far east side of town. On the concrete steps leading to the dirt path, the Kiwanis Club once etched the names of its members. Dad points out the names of my mother's male relatives, the Petersons and Sargents. He tells me that my great-grandfather, John Peterson, was on the City Council. I wonder whether my mother walked this path and if she felt pride in her ancestors.

When we get to the top, we see a bird's-eye view of Red Wing, the power plant edging the river, red brick buildings repetitively dotting the view. Below us is the rootbeer-colored Mississippi, its surface pockmarked. Limestone cliffs encircle this part of Red Wing, their striations of yellow, orange, and brown bringing to mind candy corn. The landscape is so different from pancake-flat Iowa, where we have recently moved.

"Somewhere over there is the chicken farm where the Sargents moved when Jean was in high school." Dad points toward the Wisconsin side of the river. "She didn't want to change high schools so she lived with relatives in Red Wing until she graduated."

"Which relatives?"

"I'm not sure. And I guess we're not going to find the farmhouse today. It looks like it may have been torn down."

We turn and descend the path, hop into our car, and head

toward a motel on Skyline Drive—the motel with the outdoor swimming pool, which will provide cheap entertainment for our family of six. I put on my modest two-piece suit with the built-in bra and seat myself along the pool's edge, my feet dangling in the water. The pool reeks of chlorine. My brothers jump lickety split into the pool where Dad is already swimming. He takes turns grabbing each of the boys and tossing them into the water.

"Come on in, Martha," Dad beckons.

"It seems kind of cold," I say, shivering a bit. The sun has gone down.

Dad gets out of the pool and hands me his towel. He sits down beside me as I put the towel around my shoulders and lean his way. We sit silently, watching my brothers play.

I keep thinking about what Tommy said: *Who was Jean Sargent?*

STRANGERS

All mothers and their children begin their relationships as strangers, navigating the distance between expectation and reality.

"That's where Martha was born," Dad would sometimes say, pointing toward Allen Hospital in Waterloo, Iowa, as we idled at a stop light. "She looked just like me when I was sleeping. That's the first thing I thought when I saw her. We knew right away she might have red hair."

I find out later that he was paraphrasing my mother's words, spoken when he arrived belatedly at the scene of my birth. I had the impertinence to arrive three weeks early while Dad was working halfway across the state. My mother drove herself to the hospital.

Every time we passed this hospital, I would stare wordlessly at this unremarkable four-story brick structure, pressing my nose against the car window, trying to place myself and my mother within its walls, giving each other our first once-over, my vision blurry, hers laser sharp.

What did my mother think when she looked at me for the first time? Was she delighted by my resemblance to Dad, or disappointed not to see herself in my face? Did she recoil at the large strawberry birthmark which stood out like a jagged flower on my scalp (which Dad has described as quite unsightly)? She must have disliked it, because it is not visible in any of my baby photos. Mother must have positioned me on my "good" side.

Did she wonder, *who is this person? Did I really give birth to her?*

Was she glad to have her body back? To no longer have to share it with a stranger? Did she welcome the severing between mother and child which happens with every birth? Did I?

***

I met my second mother at a toy counter in Woolworth's. She sold me a doll, which must have seemed like a weak replacement for my missing baby brother. Soon this woman became a replacement for my first mother.

Myra never told me her first impressions of me. Did she think I was cute? Did she think she could learn to love me as a daughter? Or did I remain a mystery, a nut she could never crack?

Since Dad often travelled for work, I spent many hours alone with Myra. Many of my early memories are pleasant. We watched *I Love Lucy* together. We ate warm meals filled with comfort food. We shopped for clothes. I helped her take care of my baby sister.

But over time we grew apart. We never developed a vocabulary to cross the bridge which divided us.

***

Some strangers are only anticipated. I waited for a birth child to bring my mother back to life by looking like her and sharing her talents. This birth child would reshape my life story, pulling it in the direction of normalcy. Perhaps such heavy expectations scared this child off. In any event, I have had to settle for the fact that it is my brothers and I who keep Jean alive. Tommy looks like her, with his opalesque eyes. Both of my brothers are musically talented, even though I am not.

***

My children's birthmothers have not arrived either.

***

Just as my mother and I began as strangers, so began my relationship with my children. Clara looked me over skeptically. *Who are you? What is happening?* She took her time. But when she attached, it was with a fierceness that surprised me. She figured out that I was the stranger she had been searching for.

With Lucas, it was as if he had never met a stranger, so quickly did he seem at home.

John and Clara

13

Crooked Lake

June 1984

I'm sh-sh-shaking, Mommy," seven-year-old Lucas shouts as he runs toward my open arms. His body continues quivering like Jello as I squeeze him close, wrapping him in a towel. "The water's too cold."

"I know," I sympathize. "I put my toe in. It's like ice." I remember my own childhood experiences of swimming in a lake, when our family would take our annual vacation to Lake Hackensack in central Minnesota to rent a rustic cabin and engage in a week of swimming and fishing. It wouldn't take long for me to turn the shade of a blueberry when exposed to the frigid waters. Lucas and I are the skinny ones in the family, lacking in insulation which would protect us from the cold.

The only time I really like to swim in Crooked Lake is July, when the water is finally warm. Then I wade in up to my waist, bend my knees, and lean back. I squint up at the sun as I begin to float, and thank my lucky stars that John and I are raising our children on this lake where we have spent so many summer afternoons.

Sitting on the sand near the shore, I continue holding Lucas in my arms. Meanwhile, John and Clara play in the water, Clara jumping from the beaten-up wooden raft, John carrying her around on his back. As I watch them interact, my body bursts with pleasure. I married John knowing he would be a wonderful father.

"Are you keeping your eyes peeled, Mommy?" Lucas asks, his shivering finally abating.

He loves this phrase, finds it hilarious. And his new favorite word is *scatological*, which in our family means using bad language. I taught him that word. He and I share a verbal facility and a sense of humor.

Lucas jumps off my lap when John emerges from the water. My eyes scan my husband's hairy chest, covered with chestnut brown curls, which never fails to set my heart to beating. Such a handsome man, my husband! He reaches into the fork of a tree, where he has left his glasses. He dries his back with Lucas' towel, shimmying his hips.

Exactly fourteen years earlier, in 1970, we came to Crooked Lake for the first time. The lake grabbed hold of us that day and has never let go.

***

"Where are we supposed to turn again?" John asks, seated at the wheel of the car borrowed from his parents. It is early dusk and we are newly in love, living together, thinking about getting married. We are driving slowly down Crooked Lake Boulevard, peering at large grassy lots in between modest houses which look to have been built in the forties and fifties.

We have driven from our home in Iowa City to Minneapolis to attend a wedding reception for our best friends. It is being held on the shores of Crooked Lake, on land which has been owned by their family since the 1920s.

"There's supposed to be an old red barn on the left. And a sign that says Walden Three."

"Why Walden Three? What's that supposed to mean?"

"It's the name of their neighborhood association. It's meant to be ironic. They're against Thoreau's social isolationism that he writes about in *Walden Pond* and B. F. Skinner's social engineering in *Walden Two*. Remember studying Skinner in our psychology class? Pam's parents came up with the name."

"There it is! The red barn." John swerves and follows a dirt road to an opening in the woods, the car crawling toward a group of summer cabins organized haphazardly like loose puzzle pieces.

"You figured it out," Ruth, Pam's mother exclaims, emerging from the gray cabin on the point, her long hair and loose caftan trailing behind her diminutive frame. She is soon joined by Steve and Pam. Steve is tall, mustached, and balding. Pam is much shorter, like both of her parents, with owlish granny glasses and fine hair falling unevenly on her shoulders. Last comes her father, Russell, wearing a Thai cap, brocaded elephants lining its perimeter. With his longish hair and graying sideburns, he looks like the college professor he is.

"Welcome to Crooked Lake," he says.

After a brief tour of our surroundings, which leaves me totally confused as to which cabin belongs to which of Ruth's cousins, we are led to a little bunk house, used as a study. We drift off to sleep amidst the smell of musty books and awaken to the piercing cry of a loon.

The next day we attend the wedding reception, a magical event featuring picnic tables which line the shores and little girls in flowered dresses helping to serve. Steve and Pam pose for photos on the dock, Pam wearing her JCPenney's wedding dress and Steve clad in a T-shirt, holding a fishing rod.

During the reception, overwhelmed by all of the new people I am meeting, I wander off, walking along the shore. I move into a wooded area, populated with red oaks, wild geraniums, and pink and yellow columbine. From my vantage point I gaze toward the water, mesmerized by the water's gentle rocking. I don't know it then, but someday we will build a house on this very land.

***

"Let's build something, Lucas," John says, plopping down into the sand. John is a man of action, always in motion. He and Lucas are mechanically inclined. Whether using Lincoln Logs, LEGOS, or sand, they can build it.

Clara runs out of the water. Her skin is more bronze than ever, requiring only a few minutes of sun before it darkens perceptibly. She looks enough like John to be mistaken for his biological daughter, given their even features and their similar body types. But there is not much chance I could have produced such a child.

"Are you ready to get dressed?" I ask. She nods, running toward the house ahead of me. "Clara and I are going in," I yell. "I'll start dinner pretty soon."

I run water for a bath and Clara jumps in. Soon she lays her head down into the water while I wash it with baby shampoo, quite a task because it has grown so long. I have never had long hair in my life, my fine hair seeming to have a limit regarding the degree to which it can stretch.

When Clara emerges from the tub, I dry her off. I sit down in a chair and Clara squeezes between my legs, her back facing me. I run a comb through her glistening hair, trying not to tug too hard. I carve a part down the middle and further divide her tresses into three sections. Deftly I weave the sections back and forth, until I run out of hair. Then I move to the other side.

"All finished," I declare. I stick my nose into her scalp.

"What are you doing, Mommy?" Clara giggles.

"I'm smelling your hair. It smells like Clara." It still has the musty smell I noticed at our first meeting.

"Let me see, Mommy." I hand her a mirror. Her head moves from side to side. "You did a good job."

"Thanks for the compliment." Before Clara, I never knew how to braid. I taught myself.

"You entertain Mommy while she fixes dinner."

Clara climbs onto the bench facing our used Steinway piano, situated near the open kitchen. According to her piano teacher, Clara has an ear for music. But I already knew this because she could hum before she could talk. I also know this because when she was four, and we were riding in the car listening to the radio, a song came on that she recognized from her piano lessons.

"But why are they playing it in the key of G? I learned to play it in C," she says. I have no idea what she is talking about, but I know it suggests precocity.

I can't even read music. My parents discouraged me from taking up a musical instrument in grade school, on the flimsy excuse that I couldn't breathe through my nose. A piano was off the table due to its expense. And I stopped taking choir when I got my first ever "F" on a music quiz in junior high. "Musical ability has skipped a generation in our family," I sometimes joke to John.

***

What I wouldn't give to hear my mother sing!

I don't think about my mother every day. Her loss doesn't rule my life. But grief has a way of unfurling itself slowly. When I do think about her, a sharp jab pulls me into a sinkhole of sadness as I struggle with regret for what might have been: my mother and daughter, sharing a love of and a talent for music.

I envision my daughter and mother sitting together on the bench, taking turns playing a melody, my mother gently helping Clara to position her hands correctly.

I want my mother to know *this* daughter, not the imaginary daughter I once desired, the daughter who might look like my mother. And for my daughter to know her.

"You sing, Grandma," Clara would say.

"And you will be my little accompanist." My mother would say as she begins to sing *Row, Row, Row Your Boat*. My mother would have known how to nurture Clara's talent, I am sure. And I might even have found some buried musical ability of my own. I shake off the weight of sadness and hoist myself, once again, out of this hole called grief.

***

"Great!" I shout periodically as I pull together a casserole, visions of Carnegie Hall dancing in my head. "I don't think you've missed a single note."

Lucas and John come in. Lucas resists taking a shower, but John talks him into it. I carry our meal down to the porch.

"We saw a heron," Lucas announces.

John adds, "It was out on the point."

"What's a heron?" Clara asks.

"Remember, I showed it to you when Daddy took us fishing. It has long legs."

John adds, "We'll see it again, Clara. It lives on the lake."

"We saw a heron when we went to the Boundary Waters too. We saw it fly off when we were in our canoe," I add. We recently took our children on their first camping trip to the Boundary Waters Canoe Area in northern Minnesota.

Looking out the windows, John thinks he sees something move, something much bigger than one of the numerous squirrels. "Look," I whisper, pointing. Between the oaks and pines, we all see a fawn, tiptoing gingerly, bending down to nibble on the brush. We watch, transfixed.

"But where is its mother?" I worry. We all move closer to the window.

"There!" Lucas points. Sure enough, there is the mother, hanging back, allowing her offspring its independence while maintaining a protective closeness. Her head suddenly turns toward the window where we are gathered, and just as suddenly, she gallops away, her little one following close behind.

"So adorable!" Clara says. "Will the baby deer come back?"

"I hope not," John jokes. "Just another mouth to feed."

The deer are notorious for destroying our flowers, chewing them down to the nub. I say. "They will be back. The baby and its mommy."

Later, when I tuck them into bed, in the room they still share, Lucas asks if I think they will hear the loon tonight.

"Maybe. I saw it and its baby on the lake this afternoon," I say. Clara mimics its maniacal cry with perfect pitch.

As I leave their room, I think to myself, "I hope this summer never ends. And that my children stay like this forever."

14

Research

October 1984

As John and I raised our children, adoption, especially international adoption, accompanied our daily lives. When we looked at our children and saw in their faces the reflection of other cultures and other races, we couldn't help but be reminded of their pasts. We enrolled both children in Korean Culture Camp. We went to events at Children's Home Society of Minnesota (CHSM). Clara joined a group of children who performed Guatemalan folk dances at the annual Festival of Nations in St.Paul.

When I began a graduate program in psychology and needed a topic for my thesis, I naturally thought of adoption. I came up with a project with the unwieldly title *The Initial and Long-Term Adjustment of Children of Korean Descent Adopted in Infancy By Minneapolis–St. Paul Area Families.* I chose Korean children because at the time their adoptions were much more numerous than those of Guatemalan children.

With the help of CHSM, I randomly chose fifty families and asked them to participate in an interview. About half agreed.

I didn't particularly enjoy this project, though. One, I have no sense of spatial direction, so driving around unfamiliar suburbs looking for a house matching an address was taxing. Two, I am an introvert. I didn't like going into the homes of strangers and asking them personal questions. Three, I have an overactive guilt complex. I felt that my study was missing something. I worried I wasn't asking the right questions. Questions that might be crucial to the future well-being of my children.

**

What in the world are you doing? I mutter to myself as I move my minivan slowly through an unfamiliar suburban neighborhood, grabbing quick glances at the address written on a scrap of paper. With relief I see that the numbers on the house in front of me match those on the paper. I park my unwieldy vehicle and grab the manila folder that contains my notes.

I walk to the front door, ring the bell. The house is big and beige, the lawn well-manicured. It is what used to be called a McMansion.

A middle-aged woman, faintly Scandinavian looking with a slender body, light brown hair, and a handsome face, opens the door.

"Hello, Mrs. Peterson?" I say. "We spoke on the phone. I'm Martha Bordwell."

"Sure, we're expecting you. Come on in. And call me Nancy."

Nancy leads me into her living room and introduces me to her husband Paul, who also appears Scandinavian, not surprising considering their last name. I perch on a couch next to a coffee table adorned with family photos, including two pig-tailed Korean girls. I accept a cup of coffee and comment on the attractiveness of the girls.

I won't be meeting these children. My study only involves meeting the parents of children adopted before they were a year old.

We make small talk. Then I begin to ask my standardized questions. I don't use a tape recorder, but rely on my notes.

I ask about the decision to adopt and about the child's initial adjustment. I ask about attachment, about the reaction of relatives, about school, about hobbies, about attitudes toward the child's cultural heritage, about expectations for the future.

Nancy's and Paul's answers mirror the answers of most of the other parents. Most adopted after experiencing infertility, although a few already had birth children. The children attached easily. A surprising majority are good students, over fifty percent enrolled in gifted programs (as is Lucas). The children are pursuing ordinary activities like dance and soccer. Extended families were welcoming, especially after meeting the child.

Attitudes about cultural heritage are a bit more diverse. Some parents embrace it while others are holding off. They want to follow their childrens' lead. One father says, "I hardly know anything about my German ancestry, so why should I expect my child to care about hers?"

In general, the answers seem rather bland. The parents are good people, trying to do their best. They strike me as sincere in their gratitude for the blessings their children have delivered to them. In one way, I am comforted by this. In another way, I am not. I want to find a problem. If I know what the problem is, perhaps I can confront it in my own children, head it off at the pass.

But two interviews do stand out. In one, a young girl is described as feeling negatively about her appearance. She doesn't want to go swimming because she doesn't want to display her skin. She insists on wearing glasses to hide her eyes, even though her optometrist thinks contact lenses would be a better solution for her vision problems. She is mean to other Asian children, calling them names.

One boy is displaying even more trauma. He has frequent night terrors, crying for hours. He becomes hysterical when his parents try to talk to him about adoption, running from the room.

I look for commonalities across these two families. The only one I find is that in both cases, the father approached the adoption rather passively. "I told her if she wanted to do this that was fine," one dad says affably, his smile tight.

"It was her thing," The other dad says.

That isn't our family's problem. John has approached parenting and adoption with gusto. Nurturing comes naturally to him. I was the one who hesitated.

One of the mothers, whose child is otherwise doing well, says it took her two years to feel attached to her child. I admire her honesty.

***

My own children are doing pretty well at this point. Lucas is as smart and affable as ever. His teachers like him. True, he is an underachiever in school. When he attended a summer program for gifted children, he was not a self-starter, never finishing the assigned project. His teachers tell me he is a follower, not a leader.

Issues of racism have been minor, as far as I know. But Lucas came home recently from first grade in tears, a rarity for him. We sat down on the couch.

"Boys on the bus made fun of me. They called me chink." He pulled on the corner of his eyes. "They made their eyes look this way."

"Do you know what chink means?"

"Chinese? I tried to tell them I'm not Chinese, but they wouldn't listen."

I ask, "What boys? Your friends?"

He shakes his head. "No. Sixth graders."

"Then they're bullies," I insist. "You know you have beautiful eyes, right? They are just jealous." He nods, moves away. "Do you want me to talk to the school?"

He shakes his head. "No."

"Let's see if it happens again. Just tell them to leave you alone if they do it again, okay?"

"Okay."

"Let's practice." I put my hands on my hips, deepen my voice. "You guys get away from me! You bullies!" I growl.

Lucas giggles. "You get away," he repeats. His growl isn't too convincing.

He goes off to play, never bringing up such incidents again. I don't know if he followed my advice, or found it wanting.

Clara is a mix of precocity and delays. She continues to impress musically, playing both the piano and the violin. She learned to read before entering kindergarten, quickly memorizing words by sight. But she is lagging behind in math and seems to have much more difficulty with abstractions than Lucas ever did. We have already hired a tutor for math, in keeping with our super-parenting tendencies.

***

I write up my study and it is praised by my advisors. They encourage me to apply to a PhD program, which I eventually do, planning to become a counseling psychologist. I put aside my thesis and decide that when I write a dissertation, I won't choose a topic so close to home. I don't write much about adoption after that.

Years later, when I decide to write this book, I revisit the literature. I study the history of both Korea and Guatemala, reviewing the oppression which created the need for so many adoptions. I also read about the circumstances which have led to the virtual cessation of international adoption in both countries.

I discover the words of the adopted, the voices I didn't hear when I did my own small study. In *The Language of Blood* I hear the voice of Jane Trenka, adopted by a family in Minnesota when she was two. I read: "How can a person, exiled as a child, without a choice, possibly fathom how he or she would have turned out had he stayed in Korea? How many educational opportunities must I mark on my tally sheet before I can say it was worth losing my mother? How can an adoptee weigh her terrible loss against the burden of gratitude she feels she has for her adoptive country and parents?"

I learn that Trenka, now living in Seoul, has been a leader in promoting the end to international adoption in Korea. She and other adoptees have been instrumental in passing a new law which requires that birth mothers be given more time and support before relinquishing a child. The law requires adoptive parents to travel twice to Korea to adopt their child, greatly increasing the cost of adoption and the length of time it takes to adopt.

I watch actress and playwright Sun Mee Chomet's performance in *How to Be a Korean Woman*, when she describes returning to Korea to be reunited with her birth mother. Reunification has become increasingly popular in Korea. I learn that Chomet's path to reunification started when she appeared on a reality show in Korea which promoted the meetings of birth mothers and their children. A woman came forward and a positive DNA test followed. I learn that Chomet's mother didn't relinquish her willingly, but that her family took her to an orphanage and that her mother tried, unsuccessfully, to get her back. I discover that this is not uncommon. I feel my body soften and tears well when, speaking of seeing her birth mother's naked body at a Korean public bath, I hear her say, "I felt like I was seeing my own future." I think of my own longing to see my mother's body.

I shake my head in disgust when I read about Guatemalan adoption in *Mamalita* by Jessica O'Dwyer. The story describes the corruption into which Guatemalan adoption descended many years after we adopted Clara as it was taken over by greedy lawyers and hired "baby grabbers" who stole children from their impoverished mothers. When I read another account by a journalist, I hold my breath as one mother rushes to find her abducted daughters before they are carried off to the United States by adoptive parents. I learn that all adoptions ceased in Guatemala in 2008 because of the corruption into which it sank.

I find these narratives more compelling than the stories yielded by my own research. But these narratives won't necessarily be the stories of my own children. Their stories are more complicated, and each one different from the other, defying simple storylines.

John and I continue to try to do right by our children. With them, we journey to their birth countries. These journeys yield unexpected discoveries that will cast a long shadow.

Kimchi pots

15

Motherland: South Korea

June 1990

I am bombarded by a deluge of sensations. Noisy crowds surround me. People are on the move, walking and talking quickly, their questioning inflection odd to an American ear. Many of the faces seem rounder and broader than typical Caucasian facial shapes, their features emphatic, as if drawn by a magic marker as opposed to a pencil. Bodies seem sturdy. The smells are overpowering: garlic mixed with peppers, the legendary fermenting cabbage called kimchi encased in ubiquitous ceramic pots. It is impossible to take everything in, especially as John and I are trying to shepherd our children through their first few minutes in this exotic land, which up to now has simply been the subject of picture books and folk tales recited at Korean Culture Camp.

We are on a tour of South Korea arranged by Children's Home Society of Minnesota (CHSM), accompanied by a group of adoptive parents and their adolescent children. John's mother, Esther, has come along also. Lucas, thirteen, and Clara, ten, trail along, wide-eyed, trying not to show their awe.

During the trip we are scheduled to visit temples, private homes, and Lotto World, the Korean version of Disneyland. We also visit the demilitarized zone (DMZ), the border between North and South Korea.

"Nobody is allowed to wear denim," our tour guide explains the day before, as he prepares us for the trip. "The North Koreans claim that denim is decadent. And all of the women must wear skirts." We have to go to a department store to outfit Lucas properly. As we board the bus, a man examines the attire of each of us, rubbing fabric between his hands.

When we arrive at the border, the guide orders, "Remember, no one should make any sudden moves. Don't even lift your hand to point." I stare nervously at the men bearing firearms on both sides of the border, monitoring our movements like hawks. I stay close to my children, ready to throw myself in front of them should their behavior cause consternation among the gun-toting soldiers. We can look across the border and see North Korea, but we are allowed no glimpse into private life there. We just see unadorned buildings stretched out in a long gray line. The ride back to Seoul is a quiet one.

Although Lucas and most of the boys treat this trip to Korea as a vacation, constantly on the lookout for video game arcades and other opportunities to goof off, many of the girls seem preoccupied with a more serious purpose. Some have arranged interviews at Eastern Child Welfare, the Korean adoption agency that CHSM works with in placing children. One girl stays close to her mother, an anxious expression clouding her face. She is hoping to learn about her birth mother and possibly her foster mother. Another girl also stays off to the side, ignoring her parents, as she studies the Korean language, constantly reviewing the flash cards she has made. She, too, is hoping for a meeting with someone who can provide answers about her past.

It is 1990, just when CHSM is changing its approach to foreign adoptions, based on the feedback from adoptive parents and adoptees that many of these children are hungry for a better understanding of their birth cultures. In many cases they want to know more about, and even meet, their birth parents, particularly their mothers. To that end these Motherland tours have begun.

Mrs. Han, the Korean social worker who had been recruited by CHSM to oversee their program, leads the tours. Her obvious commitment to Korean adoption has garnered her a great deal of trust among adoptive parents. She and her husband have adopted a Korean-born son.

"Do you think you would like to find information about your birth mother?" we ask Lucas before the trip.

"I don't care," he answers. At this point in his life he is preoccupied with graduating from sixth grade, entering junior high. He has parties to go to, friends to play with, forts to build, video games to conquer. Birth mothers, especially birth mothers you have been told you would never see again, appear to be an unwelcome intrusion.

Although uncertain of what to do, we ask Mrs. Han to find information about our son's foster and birth family prior to the trip. We receive a letter from the agency saying that his foster family has not responded to a request for a meeting. And little information has been found about his birth family. We are given the name of the town where his father grew up, a suburb of Seoul, and the name of the hospital where he was born. The person writing the letter apologizes repeatedly, but nothing can be done. We have mixed feelings about this dead end, not sure if we will just be opening a can of worms if we pursue it further.

***

Toward the end of our trip we visit a home for unwed mothers. We parents sit on the floor in a circle. Many of the girls sit next to their mothers while the boys congregate toward the back. We are soon joined by the pregnant women living in this home who are preparing to relinquish their unborn children. They kneel beside Mrs. Han.

Mrs. Han, acting as facilitator and interpreter, asks the would-be mothers if they want to say anything to the families. Like dominos, each begins to cry as one-by-one, they speak.

"Will my child forgive me?" Mrs. Han translates.

"Are you okay?" asks another.

"I am so sorry," gasps a young woman, her belly so large she appears ready to give birth.

I lift my Kleenex to my eyes as I hear the Americans around me join the weeping. I look around for Lucas, who looks stricken, but is not crying. Yet. I turn to Mrs. Han.

What is happening here? I silently question her. Our children are being asked to comfort these women. Shouldn't it be the other way around? I feel ashamed that I have led my unsuspecting son into this trap.

But I trust Mrs. Han. Maybe Lucas needs to see this. Maybe he needs to know how wrenching it must have been for his birth mother to give him up. I'm not sure.

The mothers mostly appear to be in their twenties, although it is hard to tell. They try to explain why they are placing their children for adoption, while Mrs. Han translates. Our children have no choice but to offer these mothers forgiveness, saying they understand, that their lives are going just fine in the United States, and that they love their adoptive parents. But one girl asks why a woman in her twenties would need to relinquish a child. She understands that teenagers are too young to be mothers, but couldn't an older woman find a way?

Mrs. Han interjects. "Korean people are unaccepting of a woman who has a child and is not married. It doesn't matter the age. And it brings shame onto the entire family." The mothers nod nervously.

"But why don't women stand up to that kind of discrimination?"

"They can't," Mrs. Han insists. "And the children are the victims. They are teased in school. These mothers don't want that for their children. They love them too much."

She translates her remarks for the mothers. They cry some more.

Lucas says little as we travel back to our hotel. His face retains the stoic expression he has worn throughout the trip. We enter our Western style hotel room. Lucas bolts into a closet, tightly closing its door.

"Lucas, please come out," I plead. "Let's talk about this." I begin to cry.

John takes over, telling Lucas we hope he is okay and to take some time if he needs it. My mother-in-law quietly rubs my back, while wondering aloud if the visit has really been a good idea. I adore my mother-in-law because she is so much like my husband, nurturing and patient. But she can't do much to help our family right now.

Clara, who did not go to the meeting with us, is mystified by the drama encircling her normally placid family. "What's going on?" she repeats over and over. I can't recall how long Lucas stays in the closet.

MISSING CHILDREN

My mother's letters end when I am about four years old, two years before her death.

I wonder why. Did she just get too busy? Did Aunt Nancy start throwing letters away? Was something bothering her?

Dad said that a year or two after Tommy's birth, she had a miscarriage. He said it was hard on her. She was in the hospital for several days.

In the last photo I have of my mother, she and Dad are on a vacation, just the two of them, in the Smoky Mountains of Virginia. After Dad died I found a postcard Mother wrote to Tommy and me, stuck in the back of his desk, the desk which had once been hers. Perhaps she put it there.

"We got Martha some pretty sunglasses today and will get Tommy a present tomorrow. We miss you," Mother wrote.

In the photo, Mother sits on a stack of logs. She is wearing brown Bermuda shorts and a matching sleeveless shirt. Her hair is shorter than I had ever seen it. She smiles shyly at the camera. At my father.

I examine the photo. Does the smile seem sadder, more tentative than those taken previously? Was she still mourning the miscarried child she lost?

I calculate that she got pregnant with David on this trip. The child she would never know.

It is a small comfort to me that, because she died suddenly, my mother never knew she was going to have to leave her children behind—that she wouldn't be around to shelter them. That they would be raised by another mother.

***

I once had a friend, diagnosed with leukemia, who died and left behind a four-year-old daughter. She never accepted that she would die. A few days before she entered a coma that would lead to her death, I told her my story, offering myself as an exhibit of a girl who had survived the loss of a mother. A woman who had turned out okay.

"Can you remember her?"

"Yes," I exaggerated to a dying friend. She didn't seem to believe me.

"Nothing good will come of me dying," my friend whispered. "I can't die." She turned her head away. As she fell asleep forever, she begged her husband and the doctors to never give up, to find a way to keep her alive.

***

The women we meet at the unwed mother's home will live for the rest of their lives without their children. The children that grow in their womb, perhaps viewed as bombs about to explode or seeds that are their responsibility to nurture, will alter their lives forever.

Like these women, my son's mother, as well as my daughter's, may rise every morning, haunted by the sound of the door closing when they left their baby behind. They may live their lives not knowing what became of their children, perhaps regretting their decision, wondering if their children are thriving, longing for news of their welfare. As I will learn later, some of these mothers will have no say in their child's removal from their care, the decision made, instead, by husbands or extended family. These decisions will be forced upon them by a social policy which shuns unmarried mothers and their children and gives all decision-making authority to men.

And I, the woman who benefited from their loss, will grapple with confusion and guilt, asking whether I am complicit in their suffering. Answers won't come easily. Perhaps there are none.

Lucas' reaction to the orphanage visit made clear that adopted children have to live with the fact that their mothers either chose, or were forced, to leave them. And that their births brought sorrow to their mothers.

Their mothers will miss them.

Lucas, Clara, and Martha with Tom and Teresa's children and their nanny Maria, Guatemala City 1992

16

Motherland: Guatemala

August 1992

T e recuerdo," the diminutive, middle-aged Mayan woman tells Clara.

"She says she remembers you." I teach her the meaning of the Spanish words.

"Mi favorita," she adds.

"She says you were her favorite." Whether true or not, it is a kind remark. Clara, age twelve, beams. We are visiting the orphanage where she spent her first six months. Oddly, Clara is wearing a hot-pink T-shirt proclaiming, "If mama ain't happy ain't nobody happy." (I know this because of the photos in our scrapbook.) This is a fashion choice I am surprised I approved.

At barely five feet tall, Clara towers over this indigenous woman, her American diet apparently having made all the difference.

When we arrived, a little welcoming party of preschoolers, looking quite dapper in navy-blue sweaters and white shorts, greeted us. They waved small Guatemalan flags, the center of the flags displaying long-tailed Quetzal birds. The kids appeared to be well fed and engaged. Mirna, the social worker who had greeted us twelve years earlier, emerged from the group. She didn't appear to have aged at all. Now she is showing us around.

"You slept in this room when you lived here, Clara," she says, as we enter a bright turquoise room lined with six cribs.

Clara giggles. "I saw the photos. And I think I know one of the boys who slept in the crib next to me."

"I think you are right. He was adopted by a family in Minnesota at about the same time you were."

Although my memories of the place are dim, my attention having been focused so much on Clara, we are pleased with what we are seeing: the well-kept lawn, the brightly painted furniture, the energetic children. We return to Mirna's office.

"Clara, do you want to show Mirna the scrap book we brought?" I prompt, handing it to her.

Clara opens it shyly, pointing out our house, her bedroom, Crooked Lake, our cat Ricky, and photos of family vacations.

"We went to Europe for a month. Dad took us to Switzerland, where he lived during high school. And this is a picture of me playing the violin at a recital."

"Clara is quite a talented musician," I brag. "She has all of these certificates."

Mirna nods enthusiastically. What must she think, as she recalls carrying away a tiny baby from her impoverished mother's hospital bed, that this same child has landed in the midst of such wealth and opportunity?

The subject of Clara's birth mother doesn't come up during this visit to the orphanage. We assume, given Guatemala's level of poverty, that finding her mother would be impossible. I regret not discussing this issue with Clara. But at the time we were as confused as most parents of transculturally adopted children. How hard should we push the issue of connection to birth family? If we push it, will we cause our children's "differentness" to be magnified? Will Clara be made to feel less secure in our family?

Because we don't know, we leave the issue undiscussed. We don't have the words. It seems safer to introduce our child to her birth culture than to her birth family.

***

We are planning to spend a month in Guatemala. Tom and Teresa, along with their three children, now live in Guatemala City. The adults lead tours for a global travel organization. We plan to spend a few days with them.

We enter their two-story house, festooned with Guatemalan weavings and indigenous furniture made of rattan and wood. When we first arrive Tom and Teresa are away leading a tour. The kids introduce us to their live-in housekeeper, Maria, an attractive young woman who is wearing a huipil decorated with enormous red flowers. Labor is so cheap in Guatemala that many middle-class families can employ household help. Maria prepares meals, does the laundry, and is treated as a member of the family. The children, fluent in Spanish, translate between Maria and us.

All five kids are old friends and quickly settle into a comfortable routine. Clara goes with Carmen to her public school. I walk with them to the school a few blocks away. Carmen carries a heavy backpack.

"What did you think?" I ask Clara when they return.

"It's way different from my school."

"In what way?"

"It's kind of dirty. Paint is peeling off the walls. And they hardly have any books."

I say, "Children have to buy their own books and carry them back and forth. And parents in Guatemala have to pay for their kids to go to public school. It's a big sacrifice for many families."

We spend five days with our friends, then take a bumpy bus ride where we are crowded in among the natives. We are headed to San Lucas, a small village located on Lake Atitlan. John is going to volunteer as a doctor at a diocese, and I am going to be his translator. We visited the diocese fifteen years earlier with Tom and Teresa.

"I hope they don't have any chickens on this bus," Clara says skeptically. We have told her about encountering passengers carrying live chickens when we were in Guatemala before. And, lo and behold, a woman climbs on with a chicken under her arm. Clara and I make eye contact, covering our mouths to hide our smiles.

***

On our first night at the diocese, a knock on the door interrupts our sleep. A woman is in labor. The middle-of-the-night call is one John and I both know well. John is tense about taking on such a responsibility in a foreign environment, he tells me. Worried myself, I can't get back to sleep. I wonder if I should have gone too, to assist with translating, but I don't want to leave the children alone at night. He returns three hours later.

"How did everything go?" I ask.

"Fine. The baby is healthy," John answers as he wearily removes his shoes. "But the mother walked for six hours to get to the clinic. And says she is going to walk back home today. I'll talk to someone at the diocese about providing a van."

When the children wake up, we tell them what their dad has been doing all night. Having grown up with a doctor father, they take it in stride. But the story about walking six hours gets their attention. Clara shakes her head.

"I'm glad I don't live here," she says. I wonder if she is

thinking about the circumstances of her own birth. I am silent, having no information to share.

***

When not volunteering, we tour the area. We climb into a small, rickety boat and wait for the weather-beaten driver to engage the motor. Quickly we gather speed, water splashing our arms and our faces. I turn my head toward the sun, briefly close my eyes as I feel its warmth. I open my eyes to the sapphire blue of the lake.

"Look, Clara!" I shout over the din of the motor. "Do you see how the huipils have changed, how the women from this next village are wearing different colors?" We peer at the shoreline, at the groups of women gathered there, getting ready to board small boats themselves, perhaps heading off to the market to sell or to buy. "You can tell from the huipils what village a woman is from."

Clara nods with mild interest but doesn't say much. Garbed in jeans from the Gap, then the prevailing fashion in Minnesota, she seems unimpressed by these women in native clothing.

We also make use of the church van. On the steep and dusty roads, we pass lines of women carrying firewood and buckets of water—their steps quick, their damp huipils clinging to their backs. They balance foodstuffs on large flat baskets perched on their heads.

We pass tiny homes made of thin slats of corn stalks which serve as walls, tin roofs atop. Chickens and an occasional cow forage in the sparse weeds nearby. When we stop, dirt-smudged children pose shyly for photos, often extending their hands to receive a few quetzales (the Guatemalan currency) in exchange for their cooperation. Their mothers sit on stoops, some holding an infant in one arm while coiling thread for weaving with the other.

I ask Clara, "Do you want to be in a photo?" She shakes her head.

Clara is growing up on this trip, right before my eyes. I watch as she seems to become increasingly self-conscious, her shoulders hunching as she walks. She seems lost in private thought, reminding me of my own entry into adolescence.

***

The summer after my family moves to Waterloo, Iowa, when I am eleven years old, I get hooked on the soap opera *Love of Life*. Myra and I watch it together.

It comes on around noon, right after we have finished our lunches of slimy baloney sandwiches and canned Campbell's soup. My brothers head back outside to play with the numerous baby boomer children swarming about our new neighborhood on West Third Street. Lisa is put down for a nap.

Myra groans as she sits down in the recliner usually reserved for Dad. A pile of clothes await folding at her side. Childish shrieks waft through our front door, which was left wide open in those days before air conditioning. The humid aroma of an Iowa summer perfumes our living quarters.

I sprawl near the black-and-white TV, all spindly arms and legs. I don't want Myra to see my face, how my mouth hangs open a little as I stare at the handsome leading men with their square jaws, limpid brown eyes, full heads of hair, and deep baritones. I don't want her to see how I blush at the kissing scenes.

Something unfamiliar is going on with me. I am starting to feel odd bodily stirrings in strange places, dreamily imagining myself to be the object of male lust—images that will remain entirely abstract for the forseeable future.

What about Myra? To where is she transported? Does she travel to a world that doesn't involve dirty diapers, dirty dishes, and dirty clothes? A life which doesn't involve raising another woman's children? Or is she reminded of her and Dad's whirlwind courtship, the summer they fell in love? Can she relate to these smitten-but-conflicted heroines, even though my dad, who has been bald since his early twenties, certainly doesn't have a perfect head of hair or big brown eyes?

"I don't know what he sees in her!" she says. Later, "They would make the perfect couple." Her remarks irritate me, interrupting my reverie. I have reached the age where much that Myra does irritates me.

The program over, I reach for the switch. Reaching into the laundry basket, Myra holds up a sleeveless dress. "Do you think this is going to fit you this year?"

I stand up, hold it up to my chest. It's well above my knees. I'm stretching out when I would prefer to be filling out. But the one good thing about my growth spurt, the spurt which has made me taller than all of the boys, is the chance to get new clothes.

Myra shakes her head. "We'll have to go school shopping. Don't know when I'll find the time."

***

We board the plane, ready to return to Minnesota.

I tell Clara, "When we brought you back when you were a baby, you wouldn't stop crying. Dad said it was because your ears were hurting from the air pressure, but I thought maybe you didn't want to leave."

Clara stares ahead.

"I'm glad I don't live here."

"Why?"

"The poverty upsets me."

"It's a very poor country," I say. "It makes me mad, because I think the government here doesn't care about the people. It does nothing for them."

"I don't like the men."

"What do you mean?"

"I don't like the way they look at me." I stare at my daughter.

She says firmly. "Women aren't safe here."

"Did something happen, Clara?"

"No, I just didn't like being stared at."

"I thought you might like being in a country where you looked more like everyone else."

"I don't fit in. I'm glad to be going back to Minnesota."

Once I wondered if we were doing the right thing by taking Clara away from Guatemala. Now I am wondering if we did the right thing by bringing her back.

TORNADOS

When our children were small, John and I were mainly tasked with keeping them alive and safe. The minute they were handed to us, we began tending to their growth, hoping to foster roots so deep our little plants could withstand transplantation from one environment to another, from one mother to another. Hoping that adversity might foster strength.

At first, tending to our children meant feeding and clothing them, so that their bodies didn't shrivel or freeze. It involved washing and changing them so their skin didn't turn red and blistery. It included remembering not to lay them on the couch, where they might fall off, and buckling them into car seats.

Later, when they become mobile, we put gates at the top of staircases so they wouldn't tumble down. We covered light sockets with plastic covers.

Keeping two-year-olds from danger was no small task, we discovered. Lucas wandered away from home once and was discovered a half hour later in a neighbor's garage, just as I was beginning to think of dialing 911 and ordering the lake dredged. At about the same age, Clara pulled the kitchen table over on herself, severing her lip so badly she would require plastic surgery. I scooped her off the floor, pressed a washcloth to her lips and ran with her to the car, rushing toward the emergency room.

When Lucas was five and Clara three, a tornado blew through our neighborhood. It happened on July 4, just as we were preparing to host a celebration. After putting both children down for a pre-party nap, I walked outside, reveling in how perfect our yard at Crooked Lake looked, the freshly clipped lawn, the blooming daylilies, the pots brimming with flowers. I happily anticipated the arrival of our friends, the chance to fire up our new pontoon boat, to swim in the lake, to march in the neighbors' annual parade.

A half hour later sirens went off. I rushed into my children's bedroom and ushered them both to the basement. There we three huddled while watching through basement picture windows as John bravely (foolhardily) rushes toward our canoe placed alongside the shore and struggles to tie it to a stake. Minutes after he brought his soaked body inside, forty shade trees on our wooded lot toppled; wires crisscrossed our lawn; plants were uprooted. When we returned upstairs, the lettuce I had been washing in the sink had blown all the way across the kitchen into the living room and was plastered against the windows. Our house escaped unscathed except for a damaged corner of the roof.

Instead of celebrating, John spent the rest of the day with the neighbor men wielding a chain saw while I struggled to keep the children away from the downed wires. For months after the tornado, I felt bereft upon returning home to our altered landscape. I missed the embrace of trees, the welcoming wave of the flowers. Eventually we planted new trees and flowers. We repaired the roof. We adjusted. And we had kept our children safe. But as they got older, tending to their growth and safety became even more complicated.

17

Storm Clouds

August 1995

"Okay, that does it!" I'm surprised to hear myself shouting, sounding unhinged. "You can't live here anymore if you're not going to do your part."

Lately I have heard too much of my own voice, too little of Lucas'. Lucas slumps in front of our computer and ignores me. He continues staring at the screen. His lips are pursed. He doesn't respond, which only adds to my fury.

"You were supposed to work on job applications today," I say. "And mow the lawn."

He stands up and walks robotically toward his room, steps quick, arms barely moving. He slams the door. It takes all of my willpower to resist following him and forcing open the door.

My son has seemed to stop maturing. He is behaving, in my view, like a thirteen-year-old in an eighteen-year-old body. My sweet little boy has evaporated behind dark storm clouds, sucked into a stormy vortex, taking with him his affectionate hugs and friendly smiles. They've been replaced by a quick temper and a bad attitude. I can't get used to his substitute. I don't want to get used to it.

Mothers lose their children in other ways, besides through death and adoption. It happens every day. When John gets home, I tell him what happened. "He's not ever going to grow up if he doesn't have to," I say. "It's been two months since he graduated from high school. He doesn't want to go to college and he doesn't have a job! We're going to have to kick him out."

"That seems too drastic," John argues. But I insist.

When we talk to him, trying to present a united front, Lucas glowers and squints, his stare unblinking. He won't answer. His silence is the way he controls the narrative.

The next day, after John has left for work, I stand at our kitchen window and watch my son carry a few boxes to the red Taurus we bought him for high school. The son I barely recognize with his frayed T-shirt, wisp of a beard, long and scraggly hair which sports a white streak down the middle, creating a look that closely resembles a skunk. If only he'd spent as much effort on his studies as he does on his hair, I think bitterly.

This must be what it feels like to get a divorce.

***

In fact, Lucas and my power struggle had started much earlier, way back in elementary school. It was just camouflaged by his affable attitude. He had always liked the social side of school, academics, not so much. Although enrolled in gifted programs, he seldom applied himself. He interpreted homework assignments as optional, setting up the perfect contrast with me; I never met an assignment I couldn't tackle. And I didn't just want my firstborn to excel academically, but to also pursue sports and other extracurriculars with the vigor with which John and I had once approached school.

But Lucas grew up in the era of video games and *Dungeons and Dragons*. He had other ideas regarding a good use of his time. As John and I grew more and more frustrated with what we perceived as his lack of ambition, he grew more and more resistant.

"You want me to be perfect so you can brag about me to your friends," he yelled more than once. "Sorry to be such a big disappointment."

He was right. We were disappointed. Just as we had once disappointed our own parents. But we waited until college to rebel.

***

I began college in Iowa City as a shy seventeen-year-old who had never been kissed. Since I had a mostly non-existent social life, graduating toward the top of my high school class was no problem. I was the model daughter, never giving my parents a moment's worry. As far as I know.

But soon after arriving at the University of Iowa, I began my own insurrection. I dropped my membership in the college Young Republicans. I made friends with a radical young woman from Kansas. I began protesting the Vietnam War. I smoked marijuana.

I changed my appearance, letting my hair grow, on my head and elsewhere. As the sixties unfolded, my skirt lengths inched upward. So did my prospects with the men on campus.

In the middle of my junior year, I enrolled in a class called Psychology of Adjustment (adjustment to what, I can't recall). In that class I came to know John.

I arrived one January morning to the huge auditorium with its steeply angled seats, surveyed the swarm of students, searching for a familiar face. I spotted the one person I knew, a cute guy with chestnut brown hair and long-lashed blue eyes behind his glasses. His first name was John but his last name I could never remember. I checked my notebook cover where

I had scribbled the name: Bordwell. Bordwell. I repeated to myself. We had been introduced by mutual friends.

"Don't you just love this class?" I said as I squeezed in next to him. "He says the most fascinating things."

"Yeah. I agree. What did you think about what he said about smoking?"

"I'll believe it when I see it."

At a time when both students and professors smoked up a storm in class, when a person could smoke in restaurants and airplanes, when one of my doctors once lit a cigarette during an exam, our professor had announced that in fifteen or twenty years smoking would be socially unacceptable. We tittered at the absurdity, the smokers among us, including John, reaching up to caress the pocket holding their packages of Marlboros or Lucky Strikes.

Although I often compare it to love at first sight due to its intensity, the truth is our relationship started slowly, as we got to know each other in our psychology class. We even had one "starter" date, during which I demonstrated my total ineptitude as a cook by serving him frozen hash browns which were close to inedible. As he picked at his soggy potatoes, he informed me that he could bake a cherry pie. I was both impressed and chagrinned. On that cold February night, no sparks were ignited between us. He didn't ask me out again.

On a sultry May evening three months after our ill-fated first date, just as seedlings were beginning to peek through the loamy Iowa soil, I had an urge to see John. I made my way to the Student Union, a place where I sometimes ran into him. Pretending to be immersed in a book, I kept one eye fixed on the doorway. And suddenly, he walked through!

I rushed up to him, my usual shyness hidden by this serendipity, and offered to buy him a Coke. He accepted my offer.

We walked and talked for hours on this unseasonably warm evening. All of my senses were electrified by the humid air wetting my skin, John's boyish good looks, the strength of his arms pulling me close when he kissed me goodnight.

Something started growing within me that night. The same was true for John. The next night he came looking for me, instead of the other way around. He invited me to his room with the ostensible purpose of studying together. I spent the night. I would never have another boyfriend.

When I moved in with John before we got married fourteen months later, Dad was devastated. He threatened to disown me.

***

I felt guilty for years about forcing Lucas to leave home. To do that to your child, especially an adopted child! But at the time I thought I was following the mantra known as tough love. And in fact, Lucas did get a job within days of leaving home and moving in with a friend. He moved back home a few months later and the following year he enrolled in college.

And, although I was blind to it then, I had both misunderstood and underestimated my son. By challenging the conformity imposed by formal education, a conformity with which I was entirely comfortable, Lucas was demonstrating an emerging character. A character which didn't value people according to their accumulation of good grades or trophies, as evidenced by his wide circle of friends. A character which modelled honesty, meaning he didn't tell his parents or teachers what they wanted to hear. And a character which was kind. When a friend became a single mother, he stepped in to offer support.

Character isn't always taught in school. It comes, in part, from family and community. In Lucas' case, it also came from within. As the future would demonstrate, my son was learning to take responsibility for his choices.

Martha's parents on their wedding day, January 19, 1947

18

My Mother's Silver

July 11, 1970

I am kneeling beneath the cherry tree where John and I have just been married, the ground littered with burgundy fruit. My short wedding dress is creeping up my thighs, the garland of daisies perched on my head beginning to slip.

Curious, I pull toward me the brown leather box that Dad has placed among the other presents. Zippers edge each side. As I pull them down the worn zippers catch a bit, then release. I slowly lift the wrinkled cover and stare at the gleaming contents.

"Your father spent the whole day yesterday polishing this, crying all the while," Myra tells me. "It was your mother's."

I lower my head, as if in prayer, turning away from the small group of guests encircling me. I continue to stare, grateful for the hair falling over my face, hiding my tears. I stay there, pretending to be engaged in study, for as long as I dare.

Finally my tears subside enough that I can actually see

what lies before me. I solemnly lift a serving spoon from its thin holding slot and turn it over. I run my thumb and forefinger over the lightly etched surface. I read the index card Dad has placed in the box. It says that my mother had received this silver, or at least the beginning pieces of a set, on her own wedding day. It was a gift from her Aunt Bertha.

Our wedding is a modest, hastily arranged affair. It is hasty because we decided to live together after college graduation and our parents hit the ceiling. But apparently I have been at least partially forgiven by my father. I am, in my hand-sewn wedding dress, receiving a traditional gift, a set of silver. I am receiving a family heirloom. A gift from my mother.

I finally raise my head and see my new husband standing near me, his lovely eyes concerned. He extends his hand my way and pulls me upward. He hugs me tight as I wipe my eyes once more and turn to face our guests.

***

Many years ago my father gave me a framed black-and-white photo of my parents on their wedding day. The two stand in front of the pulpit at the Methodist Church in Red Wing where they were married in 1947. Their bodies are framed by large bouquets of carnations and gladiolas.

Mother looks prettier than I have ever seen her. Her light brown hair hangs slightly below her shoulders, a dark tricornered headpiece perched atop her head. Her short-sleeved, street-length dress emphasizes how slender she is, how tiny her waist. On the bodice of her dress are sequins. She wears long, latticed dark gloves.

Dad is slightly taller than my mother. Despite his receding hairline, he is handsome, with high cheekbones, straight teeth, a ruddy complexion. Pinned to his suit is a single carnation.

They were married the day after Dad graduated from

college. Mother had already graduated while Dad was away serving in the Air Force during World War II.

Their ceremony was simple. The church wedding included only her and Dad's immediate families. On Dad's side, his mother, youngest brother John, and Nancy came. His father and oldest brother couldn't leave the family farm.

A small reception was held at Jean's parents' home outside of Red Wing. I have another photo that shows my two grandmothers balancing tiny tea cups on their laps, smiling broadly. Soon my parents would leave for Illinois, where Dad's job was waiting. I don't know if they had a honeymoon.

I wish I could have attended my parents' wedding. In fact, I wish I had known them when they were young, when their whole lives lay before them. Sometimes I wish I was their peer instead of their daughter. Because children never know their parents as well as their friends do. I long to know them as they once were.

Dad told me he met my mother when he and his roommate at the University of Wisconsin habitually ate their meals at the Methodist Student Center, where my mother worked. In fact, his roommate dated her first.

Dad introduced me to this roommate years later, when both were old men. Don took me aside and said, "Did you know your mother was a wonderful dancer?" No, I didn't. My father certainly never danced.

I looked at this stranger with awe, thinking, "You knew my mother! You danced with her!"

***

Holding the box of silver in my arms, I approach my father. "Thanks, Dad. You can't imagine how much this means to me."

Dad wipes his eyes. "It was Bertha's idea, to get us the silver. I think she hoped, since Jean and I both had college educations, that we would be upper class. I can't remember how your mother chose the pattern. But Bertha would give us a new place setting every year on Jean's birthday."

"Did you ever use the silver, Dad?"

"Very, very seldom."

I press for details. "Can you remember a time you used it?"

"I really can't. I think your mother thought we would use it more once you kids got older."

***

That night, after all of the guests are gone, I open the box of silver again. I remove a fork. I run my fingers down the surface. I wonder what to call the six-petalled flowers that cling to the edge, gradually disappearing as the handle of the fork narrows. I return the fork to its slot.

I count. Seven knives. Seven spoons. Seven forks. Plus serving pieces. I remember that my mother died a month after my parent's eighth wedding anniversary and two days before her thirty-fourth birthday. I wonder, did Aunt Bertha have an eighth place setting ready to give Jean? Instead she boarded a train on my mother's birthday, on the way to her funeral.

This silver is proof of my mother's presence at my wedding. But it is also a reminder of her absence. It is evidence that my mother knew me. And it is evidence that she has disappeared. The clanging of this silver is a reminder of my mother's voice. And that she has been silenced. The silver is a symbol of nurturing. That it has been put away for so long suggests deprivation. Its solid strength empowers me. The reminder of my loss weakens me. It is an indulgence, but its singularity, the only tangible gift ever from my mother, speaks of necessity. It is a surprise. It feels inevitable. It is a clue to who my mother was. It is a mystery. It raises questions. It is an answer. It is a connection.

Sometimes I wonder if my mother ever showed me the

silver. I wish I could remember. But one day I will show the silver to my daughter. And promise that I will give it to her some day. Perhaps on *her* wedding day.

And I do use the silver.

Fabric from Guatemala

19

Fraying Threads

September 2002

It is a late summer afternoon. Clara and I are belted into our Toyota Camry, heading east toward St. Paul, travelling down a homely highway cluttered with strip malls and franchise gas stations. I wear a denim skirt and a colorful blouse purchased on our family visit to Guatemala ten years earlier. Clara, who hates skirts and wouldn't be caught dead in a huipil, wears a T-shirt and jeans. She is twenty-two, her thick hair pulled into a ponytail behind her neck, her chocolate skin smooth. I am in my early fifties, still thin, my red hair fading to a dull blond, wrinkles beginning to pool into valleys around my eyes and mouth. Clara is living at home, having moved out once or twice and then returned, disappointing herself and John and me.

She and I are on our way to view an exhibit of Guatemalan textiles, a hopeful mother-and-daughter outing. It is being held at a small local college. As we near the exit, I am a little frazzled, as I usually am when confronting unfamiliar territory. I am not sure which way to turn.

"I'm going to massage school," Clara announces with a mixture of bravado and apprehension. "I met with financial aid yesterday and they say they will give me a loan for twenty thousand dollars."

My hands grip the steering wheel as I nearly career off the road, having had no warning of this declaration. Clara has been working in a pet store, being trained as a groomer. I think such a direction suits her well. She has a way with animals.

"Clara, you can't spend that much money to become a massage therapist," I snap. "They don't earn that much. If you signed a loan you have to get out of it."

Clara slumps and begins to cry. "Everything I try to do you criticize. You always have to ruin my plans."

"But why didn't you talk it over with me and Dad?" I plead.

"I wanted to figure it out for myself. But you always have to butt in."

I clam up, thinking that I just can't win with this girl. Depression begins to thread through my body like a hot flash. I assume our day is ruined. "I'm sorry," I mutter. "We'll talk about this later."

Somehow I find the building. When I park I wonder if Clara will refuse to get out of the car, like she might have done when she was a teenager. But she emerges, while keeping as much distance between me and her as possible. I sneak a glance her way, relieved to see that she has stopped crying. I lurch from one entrance to another as we seek the exact location, the hot sun piercing my skin. Clara follows behind.

We enter. I smile nervously at the young receptionist. She eyes Clara and me. I'm convinced that she is wondering about our relationship, sensing our tension.

We view the show separately, keeping a wide berth, the

display vitrines serving as walls of division. I struggle to focus on the ornate huipils, labelled with melodious-sounding names of Guatemalan villages, like Huehuetenango (way-way-te-nang-o) and Chichicastenango (Chee-chee-cast-a-nang-o).

My tangled web of emotions clamors for attention. Hurt and helplessness are present. But anger at myself, for not holding my tongue, takes center stage.

You didn't handle that well. Why couldn't you have waited until we get home? I berate myself.

I am also angry at Clara. Did she really sign a loan? It will just be money down the drain like other ill-considered educational and career paths that have been abandoned.

I sneak another glance at my daughter. She is looking at a display, her back turned to me. Her shoulders are straightened defiantly. I imagine her thoughts.

What a bitch! I can't wait to get away from her. She doesn't know what she is talking about. She doesn't support me when I need it. I'll show her.

She retreats to a bathroom. When she emerges, I ask brightly, "What do you think?" No answer. A shrug. "Remember when we saw some of these patterns in Guatemala?"

"Not really. Can we go now?"

***

After I left home for college, Myra's and my relationship turned increasingly frosty. The first time I came home for a weekend she complained that I left my shoes on the stairs. I was appalled at her pettiness, hanging onto my irritation for years, until I had my own adult children living at home.

We disagreed about how she was raising my sister, who was beginning to resist going to school. I proffered advice. It didn't go well.

Myra complained I wasn't keeping my apartment clean enough, that my hippie-type clothes weren't flattering.

Beneath the surface, many of our fights were a fight for my father's favor. In my disputes with my parents, I always gave Dad the benefit of the doubt, but showed no such leniency toward Myra.

Dad and I were both passionate readers. We liked to talk about politics and about history. I loved hearing stories about his childhood on the family farm, about his shenanigans with his four brothers. I had little interest in Myra's past, finding it unrelated to my own. No wonder she was jealous.

And I was jealous too. Although she hated to travel, Myra insisted on accompanying Dad wherever he went. She didn't seem to like staying at our house on Crooked Lake, preferring to stay in a motel. Once when Dad came alone to help John fix the roof after a storm, she called as soon as he arrived, saying she was sick. He turned around and went home. I was furious, seeing this as a transparent effort to keep me and my father apart.

Dad didn't encourage our rivalry, staying mostly above the fray. But when push came to shove, he was loyal to Myra. And although she wasn't perfect, she also wasn't evil. I think he made the right call.

Myra and I never directly discussed the emotional bruises she acquired as a stepmother, nor did we address the wounds of my maternal loss. We didn't discuss our grievances. We didn't have the words.

I yearned for Jean, sure that she and I would be friends, would get along. I was a living embodiment of my mother, wasn't I? The same blood flowed through our veins. She would be good humored about Dad's and my closeness. She would probably be partial, herself, toward my brothers. But not too much.

When your mother dies young, you can make up your

own stories. You can turn your "real" mother into a saint and turn the stepmother into a scapegoat.

But Myra was the woman who stepped in to mother me and Tommy, bewildered children who had lost their first mother. She was the one who had to raise teenagers and who had to navigate the increasingly complicated web that ensnares mothers and daughters.

It never occurred to me to solicit her advice when my own mothering became so complicated.

***

As Clara and I drive home from the exhibit, silence hangs in the air. I don't trust myself to say the right thing, whatever that is. At first I don't say anything. Neither does Clara. But finally I barge ahead. I try to find the words.

"I know you want to find the right career, Clara," I venture. "You are at a really hard age, when you don't know much about your future. It's a scary time." She doesn't answer. I keep talking.

"I was pretty scared when I was your age. It's true I had Dad, but you know, we were just married. We didn't know each other that well. Sometimes I wondered if we were going to make it. We were so young. We didn't always communicate very well." And I missed my Dad, our relationship strained at the time.

Why are you talking about relationships? I ask myself. I refocus on jobs.

"And I wasn't that thrilled with my job. I wasn't sure being a teacher was right for me."

Clara remains silent. Should I broach the subject of adoption? Should I ask her if she feels more alienated from her parents, especially me, because of adoption? Did she think of her birth mother as she wandered the gallery with the mannequins dressed in Guatemalan clothing? Did she wonder about her lost mother, imagine that she would be more sympathetic? Did she place this mother on a pedestal much as I have done with my own birth mother? Did she long to know her mother loved her?

"I'm sorry if it seems like I'm not supportive, Clara. That's how I felt about my stepmother, that she didn't support me because she didn't understand me. I never wanted that to happen between you and me. But that happens with lots of mothers and daughters."

Clara is leaning against the door, as if she wants to escape this conversation. We are like a couple on opposite sides of the bed, turning away from each other. But then she says. "I don't want to be poor, Mom."

"Of course you don't. But why are you afraid of that?"

"Hispanics are poor."

"Some are. But you will never be poor, Clara."

"People don't respect Hispanics. I get followed in stores."

"I never knew that. That's terrible." I struggle with what to say next. "How do you handle it?"

"I don't go back."

"I'm so sorry if racism is making your life more difficult, Clara."

"You've never had to deal with racism."

"No. I was bullied in school sometimes. But never racism."

"You don't know what it's like. Nobody I know does."

"You're right."

What a tangled web of knots my family's life has become. I feel my head exploding as I try to mentally untangle the different threads of race, school, adoption, and missing mothers. I yearn for a time in our lives when life was simpler. But was there ever such a time?

RACE AND PRIVILEGE

When Clara described the way in which her race and ethnicity has impacted her life, I experienced a visceral feeling of anxiety, as if I had always known that racial realities were bubbling beneath the surface of our family's life, ready to erupt at any moment. I feared the moment when John and I would be called to atone for the casual way in which we approached inter-racial adoption, so blithely shifting all of our family identity from Caucasian to Caucasian-Korean-Guatemalan. Now I knew, that for Clara, these issues weren't simmering below the surface at all. They erupted constantly.

I have read that in order for white people to deal with race, they first need to come to terms with their own racial identity. This is difficult because those who are a part of the dominant culture, unlike people of color, are seldom called upon to explain their identity. They take it for granted. They don't describe themselves as White, whereas they tend to describe others as African-American or Hispanic, seeing their own race or cultural identity as a given they can take for granted.

In addition, if racial identity is honestly examined, this examination can't help but be imbued with shame, because of the way in which white people of European ancestry formed this country by displacing and subjugating Native Americans and by enslaving African-Americans, who they stole from their birth continent. More recent history points to racism directed toward Asians as, for example, when the United States occupied Korea after World War II, participated in the decision to divide it into two nations, and then created conditions that directly led to the international adoption of South Korean children. The mixed-race children of American servicemen were the first children sent abroad to be adopted.

Shame is different from guilt, because guilt implies that something can be done to right a wrong or that the problem might be solvable. Shame invokes feelings of helplessness and resignation. And it is not just oneself who is complicit in wrongdoing, but the entire group with which one identifies: one's parents, one's ancestors, one's friends and associates. One can argue that the blame belongs to people who lived in the past, but that doesn't change the fact that a white person continues to benefit from the oppression of other races and ethnicities.

When one asks children of a different race to form bonds with families representing the dominant culture, what are the implications? What is it like to be asked to abandon one's birth culture and to instead identify with another culture? Does this risk making such children outsiders wherever they go? Does it transfer shame onto them as they grapple with divided loyalties and the privilege which their family ties offer?

Are we, their adoptive parents, no different from our European ancestors, who stole land from Native Americans and exploited African-born workers to further our own goals?

Can it be argued that we stole children from other races and cultures to get what we wanted: children to raise as our own?

I don't know if my children are capable of articulating their racial identities any better than I am. They take certain realities of their lives for granted. True, Clara expressed a fear that she might be poor because she is Hispanic, but the reality is that because her adoptive parents have generous financial resources, she will never be poor, unless that is her choice. Does her first-hand knowledge of white culture advantage her when it comes to dealing with racism. Or, since she has been somewhat protected from it, is she less prepared to address it. James Baldwin has argued that white people shouldn't raise children of color because they don't know how to teach their children "to be despised." But how is that a positive childrearing attitude? If they are instead taught to expect respect, are they better off?

Other adoptees, such as a woman who is quoted in a New York Times article from January 14, 2015 about international adoption, argue that it simply isn't normal for children to be raised by people of a different race. But that reasoning has its limits. Until recently, it was illegal in the United States for persons of different races to marry. The primary reasoning argued that it wasn't natural. Today we have had a president who is the product of a mixed-race marriage. Persons of mixed race are prevalent and prominent in our culture.

It is too late for John and I to reconsider our decision to adopt our children. The best we can do is listen when they choose to share with us the feelings they have about adoption, culture, and race. We can validate the way in which their lives have been made more difficult due to the decisions we made long ago, while identifying what we can do in the present to respond to these difficulties. We can recognize the ways in which values which we tried to teach in our home, such as honesty, responsibility, and empathy, might arm them against racist attitudes. We can ask, but we can't answer for them, whether they feel their personal experiences allow them deeper and wiser insights when it comes to race relations and white privilege.

Demographic trends in the United States suggest that by 2050 white people will be in the minority. Although currently we all are experiencing a backlash against this forecast, John and I hope it comes to pass. Our pasts were formed by the choices of our European ancestors. But our future belongs to our children. Our loyalty lies with them.

20

Reverse Migration

June 2005

I stand in front of the stove in our kitchen, my arm forming circles as I stir the beef bulgogi, its aromatic combination of soy sauce, brown sugar, and garlic a gift to my nostrils. I take in a deep breath.

John is at the sink, washing the leaves of lettuce he has grown himself. We will wrap the bulgogi in the lettuce.

"Do we still have kimchi?" I ask John. He moves toward the refrigerator, bends low, and in a minute pulls a jar containing the Korean staple from the back. He raises it triumphantly.

I scowl. "Is it still okay?"

He sniffs. "It's fine. Kimchi is meant to last forever."

"I can't remember the last time we used it," I say.

"When I lived in Korea I ate kimchi every day. And rice," Maya, Lucas' college girlfriend says, "I love it." She and Lucas are seated across from us on high stools.

John nods. "I do too. Can't get enough of the spicy red pepper."

"I guess I better develop a taste for it," Lucas says.

"You can start now," I say, retrieving a bit from the jar and placing it on a spoon in front of him. He reaches for the spoon and raises it very cautiously to his lips.

Now twenty-eight, Lucas has grown into a good-looking young man, slender but muscular, five foot seven, the same height as John and I. Maya is petite, with the muscular arms and legs of the champion cheerleader she was in high school. She is adopted from Korea and spent a year in Seoul, where she reconnected with her birth parents.

"So have you decided when you are going to leave?" I ask Lucas.

"In September, after I graduate."

Maya rolls her eyes. Lucas was supposed to graduate from college in June, but my late-blooming son didn't quite make it. One more credit to complete. We're just happy he is going to graduate at all.

"I'm going earlier, maybe in July. I can't wait to see my birth mom again. Now that my Korean is so improved."

"I think it's so great that Lucas is going to teach in Korea," I enthuse. "He'll learn so much about the culture by being there for an extended time."

Maya adds, "It will help him with his Korean too."

Lucas and Maya met at a Korean language class at the University of Minnesota during a college career marked by many fits and starts. He worked for a year after high school, went to college for three years, dropped out, started over. Although he had previously never made much of an effort to form friendships with Asians, he got involved in the Asian Student's Association at the University, where he made friends with many Koreans, some adopted, some being raised by their Korean parents. And now he has decided to get a job teaching English in a school in Seoul.

"I'm not so sure," Lucas says. "I'm not that good at languages."

"You just have to live there," Maya insists.

"It's so cool you found your parents, Maya. Both parents! That has got to be unusual," John says. Maya was born the youngest child in a large Korean family. Her parents had concluded they simply couldn't afford another child so had placed her for adoption.

Maya smiles. "Yeah, I feel lucky it worked out."

I hesitate, then say to Lucas, "Do you think you will try to find your birth mom?"

"You know Mom and I would totally support that," John adds. "I hope you don't have any reservations about our feelings being hurt."

"No, I know you'd be fine with it. But some of the things I've heard..." He looks at Maya.

"My birth mom can be pretty demanding. When I met her for the first time she asked for a key to my apartment. I didn't know what to say so I gave it to her. But then she started coming over all of the time and even wanted to sleep in the same bed with me. That kind of thing, mothers and daughters sleeping in the same bed, is common in Korea. So finally I asked for my key back and she was really offended."

I stop stirring. "I didn't know that was a part of the culture." I look at Lucas. "What a complicated decision to have to make."

"I don't know how much contact I'm up for so I don't want to just rush into a meeting, even if I can find them," Lucas says. "I don't think it would be fair to my family in Korea."

Maya's voice is confident. "I know Lucas will decide to find his birth mom once he has been in Korea for awhile. I am going to help him do it. Searching was the best decision I ever made."

I look from Maya to Lucas, feeling a twinge of alarm. Take it from me—Lucas doesn't respond well to pressure, I want to warn Maya. Does she get that about him?

"It's good that you are going to take your time making a decision, Lucas," I say. "You've always been good at looking at all sides of a situation."

Until this moment, I always thought it would be good, for us and for him, if Lucas searched. Having information about his birth family might help us understand Lucas better and satisfy our curiosity about his past. But given his hesitancy, I begin to have qualms of my own. Faced with the real possibility, I am conflicted.

A rush of questions washes over me. What if Lucas finds Korean culture more to his liking? What if he decides to live forever among people of his own race? What if he finds his birth mother or father and he decides they are soul mates? Where will that leave me and John?

"I'm going to set the table outside," I say, grabbing a tray full of plates and silverware. "I'll be right back."

Hurriedly, I descend the stairs. I take a deep breath as I push open the door. I put the tray on the picnic table and keep walking toward the lake, toward the same place where I stood years ago, contemplating Lucas' imminent arrival from South Korea. As I near the shore, I wrap my arms around my body, the wind chilling my torso even though it is early summer. We are in the midst of a drought, so the water level is down. Slimy green algae clings to the surface. Parched, cracked earth appears where water normally flows. A solitary mallard glides through the muck.

What does Lucas expect to find, want to find, in Korea? Does he know?

What do I want? As I have become more aware of how race and culture have impacted my children, I have committed myself to support their choices without defensiveness. But that doesn't mean it is going to be easy.

I want my son to find his place in the world, wherever that is. I want to let him go as long as he lands somewhere else where he feels he belongs and where he has relationships. I just don't want him to wander aimlessly through life, never feeling a sense of belonging anywhere or with anyone. No one wants that for their child.

But I also want him to ultimately choose me and John. Because I will miss him if he doesn't come home.

I close my eyes tightly, trying to obliterate such thoughts from my consciousness. I assure myself that the winds that buffeted our relationship a few years ago have subsided considerably. Of course he will come home.

You're being selfish, I admonish myself. *You have to let whatever happens, happen. This is not about you.* I continue watching the lonely mallard push through the algae.

You can't control your thoughts and feelings, but you can control your behavior, I lecture myself, repeating a line I frequently use with my psychology clients.

I turn back toward the house. No one seems to have noticed my absence, the conversation having switched to the process of finding English teaching jobs in Korea. I stand behind Lucas, who is still seated on a stool. Lightly I place my hands on his shoulders and squeeze. I don't want to let go.

But he needs to take the next step of his journey alone.

JOURNEYS

Our lives comprise a series of journeys, some literal, some metaphorical.

When I awoke that February morning in 1955 and traveled to my parents' bedroom, I traveled from one world to one dramatically altered. For the rest of my life I would need to find my way without my mother's guidance. It has both frightened and inspired me. It has given me a taste for solitude.

Throughout my childhood our family traveled annually to Red Wing. Within that city's limestone walls I searched for messages about my mother. I knelt at her gravesite and put my ear to her tombstone, listening for her voice. I sat among her relatives and studied family traits. I decided the Sargents possessed a kind of stillness and, for want of a better term, a goodness. Traits which I have sometimes been told I display myself.

As an adult, I have continued to visit Red Wing, placing flowers on my mother's gravesite, stopping in at the Sargent

Nursery to catch up with my cousins. By taking this drive down Highway 61, I honor the mother I can't really remember. I climb Barn Bluff, picking wildflowers, wondering if these same flowers bloomed when she was alive. I look down upon the Mississippi, proud that my mother grew up near its shores. I imagine that she once stood in my place, that her eyes saw what I am seeing.

***

As young adults, John and I went to Crooked Lake to our friends' wedding reception. We came back with more than we started with—a decision to marry. And although we were oblivious at the time, we also found the home where we would raise our children, on the lake's protective shores.

***

I never journeyed through pregnancy. Not all journeys are possible.

***

Just as I have travelled most of my life without my mother, my children have had to navigate without their birth mothers as guideposts. They were left in the care of strangers almost from the beginning. And while they were journeying away from their origins, John and I were heading their way, until our lives intersected and we became a family brought together by accident and loss.

John and I have travelled to our children's birth countries repeatedly, sometimes with them, sometimes separately. We have embraced our duty to know these countries, because of our love for our children.

When Clara went to Guatemala when she was twelve, she came back with a new body, a body advancing into womanhood. But she also lost her innocence. She could no longer view Guatemala as a magical country, the home of her people. The plight of her ancestors lost its romance, instead replaced by images of deprivation. And she learned that not all men were trustworthy, like her father and her brother. She lost whatever wanderlust she ever had, feeling safest at home.

***

Lucas was able to go back to Korea, despite the palpable anguish he felt after visiting the unwed mothers' home. Once I asked him what he remembered about our visit there. I reminded him that he hid in the closet after we came back to the hotel. He looked at me with a blank stare.

"I don't remember that," he said.

But Clara remembered. "I kept asking you what was going on. But no one would tell me," she said. "Not even Grandma."

Perhaps that is a difference between my two children. Lucas was able to forget, to repress, while Clara was not. When Lucas goes to Korea, he will definitely come back with more than he left with.

***

Some journeys are a choice. My children had no choice when it came to leaving their birth countries. But they have chosen, so far, not to travel to find their birth families.

21

Searching

November 2013

Clara's dining room table is piled high with unopened mail, assorted keys, and objects which were in the exact same place the last time I visited. Seated at the table, I pick up a lonely fork and begin fiddling with it nervously while I survey the room. Across from me, against the north wall, sits a lengthy aquarium, one big fish flitting among a school of small striated fish. On the other walls are an embroidered mola of an abstracted parrot, which used to belong to John and me; a Guatemalan machine-made weaving featuring marimba players; and a poster of Aaron Rogers, quarterback of the Green Bay Packers.

The poster and the aquarium are reminders of Carl, Clara's boyfriend of four years, who recently moved out. Carl, with a last name as Scandinavian as lutefisk, had refused to commit to marriage. Over time, his attitude had corroded trust between the two. Clara seems to be weathering the breakup fairly well. But it is hard to tell, as Clara is a very private, quiet person.

I always feel like grabbing a vacuum cleaner when I visit. Benny the cat is a very pretty boy, but he too leaves vestiges everywhere, in the form of orange hair. It is hard for me to find a place to sit which won't leave my bottom coated with fur.

"How can you find anything?" I have said more than once, much against my better judgment. It seems I can't escape my namesake—Saint Martha, the Patron Saint of Housework.

"I just don't care about housework like you do Mom," Clara retorts. "I'd rather do other things."

She is in the midst of making herself a vegan smoothie. Veganism and animal rights are passionate causes for her. She never eats or wears animal products. Belatedly remembering this, I kick my leather purse under my chair. "That smells good. What is it?"

"A basil smoothie."

"You're putting basil in a smoothie! That's what I smell! But I wouldn't think it would go in a smoothie."

"Taste it."

She brings over her glass. I inhale the pungent aroma slowly, take a sip. Frankly, I like the smell better than the taste. "Interesting. Like pesto a little. It makes me think of summer. Why don't you email me the recipe?"

"Sure."

She goes back into the kitchen. I wish she would sit down when I visit. Her busyness strikes me as avoidant. Self-protective.

I know what Clara wishes, besides that I would keep quiet about her housekeeping. That John and I would become vegans—that we would embrace a value so important to her. Thus far, we haven't made that leap.

"Clara," I begin, my voice a tad higher than usual because I want to tell her about something we haven't talked about before. "Do you remember Maria and Susanna Stevenson? They were both adopted from Guatemala. Maria is about your age."

She looks up from where she is wiping her kitchen counter, with an expression of interest. "A little. Didn't they live up north somewhere?"

"Yeah, near Bemidji."

"Why do you bring them up?" Suspicion in her voice.

"I was talking to their mom recently. She told me something I didn't know. She said it is quite possible to search for birth mothers or families in Guatemala now."

"How do you do that?" Clara's shoulders lift and straighten. She sounds as surprised as I was.

"She gave me the name of a woman in Guatemala who conducts searches. I guess everyone in Guatemala has an ID number, even people in rural areas. So it is easy to match ID numbers if a person's birth records contain that information. And Mirna from the adoption agency keeps all of those records."

"Even poor people have IDs?"

"Everyone."

"Did Maria search?"

"Yes. The family worked with the woman I told you about. Maria met her birth mother and some extended family, like aunts and cousins. She also has a brother."

"They went to the mom's house?"

"I think so. This woman who searches—her name is Mari—first finds the family. She tells them she has information from the United States which most people accept because so many have relatives living in the States. She figures out if the woman is the actual mother and then tells her her birth child would like to meet her."

"How does she make sure she has the right person?"

"Well, I guess she doesn't use high-tech methods like

DNA. Kathy said she just talks to the mother and can tell by the emotion she shows and the questions she asks."

"Then what happens?"

"She brings the adopted person to meet the family, if there is an agreement. Sometimes the adoptive parents come to the first meeting, sometimes a second is arranged. I'm sure sometimes they don't come at all. The adopted person gets to decide."

"So how did Maria handle it?" Clara asks softly.

"Her mom isn't sure. Maria is pretty quiet. Kathy thinks she has mixed feelings. But she stays in touch with her brother through Facebook."

Silence.

Clara asks, "How was her mom doing?"

"I guess she was quite poor," I say. "But some of the relatives were getting along better."

A pause.

"Have you ever thought of looking for your birth mom, Clara?"

"No. She's probably dead." She turns away, pulling dishes from her dishwasher.

"She may not be dead. After all, she is younger than I am."

"I thought people lived shorter lives in Guatemala."

"That's true. But even if she is dead you may have more family."

"I'm not really interested, Mom. Too much time has passed."

"That's fine," I blurt. "But anyway, Dad and I are planning to visit Guatemala next winter. Would you like to go with us?"

"Where are you going?"

"Antigua. It's a nice, colonial town about an hour's drive from Guatemala City. Very safe. Dad, Lucas, and I visited there before you were born. That's when we decided to adopt a baby girl from Guatemala." Clara ignores this cheery aside.

"I don't really have any interest in visiting Guatemala."

"Never?"

"I don't think it is safe for women. And the poverty upsets me."

"You wouldn't feel safe there, even if you were with us?"

"No, men treat women disrespectfully in Guatemala. Even worse than here."

"And there is a lot of poverty, I know," I agree.

"It's too overwhelming for me to see."

"Okay."

Clara, who has remained standing in the kitchen, turns her back again, putting her smoothie ingredients into the refrigerator.

"I'm not really interested in looking for my birth mom," she says again. The refrigerator door makes a sucking sound as it slams shut.

***

We're at a piano recital. Clara, age four and one of the youngest performers, is seated in the front row, next to other students she doesn't really know. She is wearing a white eyelet dress festooned with red ribbons, which contrast dramatically with her hair and skin. When it is her turn to play, she performs flawlessly. The applause is loud and long. John and I burst with pride. She sits back down. The students are arranged in order of age, and there are a lot of them. She turns my way, her lip starting to quiver. I wave, smile encouragingly. As the students jump up and down to perform their pieces, she keeps turning, tears starting to fall. I don't know what to do. I don't want to disrupt the recital. Finally, she bursts from her seat and charges through the aisles into my lap.

"I was lonely," she whispers. I dry her tears.

***

Clara and I continue to make small talk as we sip our

smoothies. I ask her about her job and about the latest happenings in the vegan community. After about a half hour, I hug her goodbye and make my way down her narrow stairs, walking to my Toyota parked along a curb. Slowly I drive through Uptown, the trendy enclave where she lives. Merging onto Highway 94, I begin the familiar drive back home, my motions on autopilot. I become aware of how sad and helpless I feel. I want Clara to have a friend with whom she can share her thoughts about our conversation. I wish Carl was still in the picture.

At least we started a dialog, I tell myself. *And I had to tell her what I found out about searches. It wouldn't be right to keep that from her.*

I somehow expected her to have a different attitude toward searching. Maybe because so much of the literature I have read states that girls are more likely to search than boys are.

I try putting myself in Clara's place. Would I want to search for my mother if I could? Bereaved children often fantasize that their dead parents aren't gone forever, that they can be found. So I think I would search if I was adopted and thought there was any possibility at all of meeting my birth mother. My curiosity would surely get the best of me.

But.

I have had the luxury of painting a beatific picture of my mother, based on the sparse but wondrous tales I have been told. I have received enormous sympathy when I describe the circumstances of her death. What could be more noble than dying in childbirth? And I have always known that she can never be found. My fantasies are merely a self-indulgent game.

I think about the helplessness in Clara's sunken shoulders as she turned away from me. She understood, as I did not, that it was too late to meet her birth mother. That they would always be strangers, separated by years, by language, by culture and by an absence of shared memories. That time has withered away their blood bond. The roots of their relationship have burrowed underground, as unreachable as my own mother's bones. Her mother's voice has been silenced. And if she went to meet this mother, out of simple curiosity, she would confront on an unbearably personal level the injustice which exists in this world. And she would be helpless to do anything about it. But it would haunt her.

I have thought that the concept of a birth mother was too abstract for Clara, and by extension Lucas, to contemplate, like childbirth is for me. But suddenly it occurs to me that I have it all backward. A birth mother is too real. She is not abstract. She is not a ghost.

Turning into my driveway, I pull the car into the garage. I don't move. I address my ghostly mother.

"I don't understand my daughter," I tell my mother. "And I don't know how to help her."

"What do you mean?'

"I don't know what it's like to have a real mother who isn't a ghost. A mother who exists but isn't present. A living mother with whom a connection has been so damaged. I don't know how to help her with that."

My mother nods. "Her mother is missing. I am missing. But you are real. You are present."

I sigh. "Is it enough?"

"I think Clara is trying to tell you that it is enough for her. But is it enough for you?"

Fountain in the central square of Antigua

22

Antigua

January 2014

I park myself on a bench in the central square of Antigua. John and I are spending part of our winter here because we love the people, the culture, and the climate. If all goes well, we may make a habit of it. John is volunteering with a medical group and I am beginning to assist a Non Governmental Organization (NGO) that helps poor children attend school.

I must be sitting in the approximate location I visited more than thirty years ago when I first witnessed the Mayan women weavers in their rose-colored huipils. Today there are no weavers. They have been replaced by huipil-clad merchants.

A woman approaches. She is wearing traje (tra-hay), the complete ensemble of a Mayan woman: a woven skirt, actually a thick-piece of fabric wrapped around her waist and held together by a wide belt; a huipil, as vibrant as a painting by Matisse; and colorful ribbons threaded through her hair. But she also wears a thin, western-style sweater and flip-flops. Her eyes are a deep brown, her skin the color of a latte. Her black hair reaches her waist. Over her arm are assorted textiles, some intricately woven in the typical Mayan way, others imported from China, that she is selling for just a dollar. In a sling on her back is a chubby-cheeked baby, a stocking cap ornamented with elephants warming his head.

"Su bebé es precioso. ¿Cómo se llama?" (Your baby is precious. What is his name?)

"Antonio."

"Y usted?"

"Me llamo Luisa." Wanting to continue our conversation, I ask Luisa about herself and her family.

"Tengo dos hijos mas."

She has two other children. Her husband works on a farm. She is twenty-six years old and comes from a nearby village.

I offer a small fee in exchange for a photo. She proudly turns to the side so that Antonio is on full display. I show her the cell-phone image, both of us grinning at the pure joy he exudes, safely pressed against the warmth of his mother's back. At this point in his life he has everything he needs: his mother.

As Luisa moves on, having sold me a sash for which I can't think of a use, I survey my surroundings. Abutting the park are one- or two-story colonial-style buildings, close to the ground because of the ever-present danger of earthquakes. The square is filled with lacy trees whose names I don't know, and lush bougainvillea, whose sumptuous colors, like smears of different shades of lipstick, never fail to make me gasp with pleasure. For as a Minnesotan, I am faced with a monochrome landscape of gray, white, and brown for six months of the year.

Beyond the park lurk slope-shouldered volcanoes, tersely named Agua and Fuego. And throughout Antigua lie piles of ruins, which the townspeople have managed to artfully incorporate into the ambience of the city. The country is too poor to cart the earthquake rubble away, so it makes do. The indigenous residents seem to adopt the same philosophy.

The square is always bustling. Gringos are common, descending on Antigua to escape a northern winter, study Spanish, buy the famed textiles, or just to live cheaply.

"My social security check goes a lot further here," one oldster confides.

Just as prevalent are the shoeshine boys, the kids selling lottery tickets, and the hawkers of textiles. I know the minute I choose my bench that a series of traje-wearing women will scurry toward me, managing to combine politeness and persistence in a way that wears down their most resistant victim.

But I am not here to buy. It seems as if I am searching for someone. For whom? For my daughter? Not my actual daughter. Clara is at home in Minnesota. But, playing a private game, I *am* looking for the woman who looks most like her. I see many young women as striking as Clara, some whose profiles are exact replicas of those carved on Pre-Columbian stelae. None, of course, look exactly like my daughter. Plus the accessories and the hair styles aren't right.

Clara just cut her usually long hair short, so short it is shaved in back. And she favors jeans and hoodies. I just can't picture her in this park.

***

Yesterday I did meet a girl who reminded me of Clara when John and I rode a chicken bus to the town of San Antonio Aguas Caliente where I intend to volunteer for the NGO. We went to meet a child we are sponsoring so that she can attend school.

The child is a charming six-year-old who sits on her mother's lap throughout our visit. Her home, which houses six children and two parents, is simple but attractive. It has a tin roof and concrete floor and a kitchen with a stove and cabinets.

"My husband designed it," the mother announces proudly.

With the leader of the NGO, we briefly stop next door to check on another child who is being sponsored. "This family is incredibly poor. They are just squatting in this space," Cindy tells us.

We knock on the locked metal gate. A teenaged girl opens it. Her bronze skin is flawless, her long hair thick, her eyes bright. Her cheeks are very round, exactly like Clara's. I can't take my eyes off of her because of the resemblance.

Her mother, displaying a toothless smile, rises slowly from a bed in the center of the room, the only furniture in the space. It is covered by tattered, dirty blankets. There are no other rooms. In fact there are no walls. The space is simply covered by a tin roof. A fire pit occupies a corner. Both mother and daughter wear worn, faded huipils.

Cindy hands the mother the card which will allow her four-year-old son to buy school supplies. "Just take it to the drugstore. The man there will give you what you need. And make sure your boy has breakfast before school," she adds. "It will help him learn."

We look around. How can this family prepare food? I ask myself. There are no cabinets, no refrigerator. We don't see any food. We see no way to get water. A hole in the corner serves as a latrine.

The teenaged girl stands behind her mother, smiling, her arms wrapped around her, looking over her shoulder at the card her mother studies quizzically. I can't tell whether either of them is able to read it. We say good bye.

"How do they survive?" I ask, shaken.

"I think she does a little weaving. The older children work selling this and that in the market. She has had seven kids by several fathers, but the men don't seem to be around. I think she may be pregnant again."

"Does the girl go to school?"

"No, she has dropped out to work. And she helps with her little brother."

We walk away, board the bus. I stare straight ahead, too preoccupied to look out the window as we pass through the village.

I remember how I stared at the shanties John, Lucas, and I glimpsed from a taxi when we arrived in Guatemala to bring Clara home to Minnesota. Since that day, I haven't thought of Clara's birth mother as often as I should have. I push away the guilt I feel, that I'm a privileged white woman who was allowed to take a child from her mother and native country, benefiting from the avarice of my European ancestors who pushed aside an entire culture and tried to replace it with their own. An ancient culture, where women wore huipils they wove themselves and taught their daughters to do the same. Where families tilled the same land for generations, until it was stolen from them. A culture that invented numerical systems and built magical temples. A culture that still survives, due to the tenacity of its people, but exists amidst the deprivation witnessed here.

I try to picture Clara's birth mother. I see an outline of her body, but not her face. I see a hotel where she still might work as a cleaning lady, her aging knees aching, her back stiff. But I can't picture her face. I assume her mother gave birth to more children. I assume none of the children have an involved father. I can't conceive of a brighter scenario.

It often seems that Clara is incredibly grateful not to have grown up in Guatemala. But I don't think of my daughter as being lucky to have avoided such a life because it came at a steep price. She lost her mother. And the culture John and I taught her to admire has lost much of its sheen. She can't bear to witness such destruction. I'm glad she wasn't here to see this family.

***

Preparing to leave the square, I focus my gaze on the fountain in its center. On each of its four sides, a long-haired maiden sits proudly, her hands cupping her breasts, from which flow streams of water. The soft murmur of the running water soothes me, just as the mesmerizing movement of Crooked Lake always does.

I stare at the maiden facing me, who seems meant to symbolize Mayan womanhood. I suddenly notice a rupture slicing through the woman's face, carving an indentation in her cheek. A crack caused by an earthquake, I suppose. A rupture reminding me of the cleaving which occurred when Clara was separated from her birth mother. A scar which can't be erased or repaired. But the maiden still stands.

As I walk past the fountain, I say my goodbyes to the nurturing maiden, looking forward to greeting her next year.

The sun is beginning to disappear behind a volcano. We are heading home tomorrow. My mind switches to other concerns. Where will John and I dine on our last evening here? What time will we rise to catch a plane?

23

Summer

September 2010

"What did you say?" I ask the young Japanese clerk. My brain must be addled after the twelve-hour flight from Minneapolis.

"The flight to Seoul is cancelled because of the typhoon. We've ordered a bus to take all of the connecting passengers to a hotel."

"A typhoon? But…" She has shifted her attention to the next passenger. Maybe I misunderstood; I tell John. He immediately approaches the counter to verify my report.

"We'd better call Yena." Gloomily, I find a phone.

"Yena, we have bad news. The flight from Narita to Seoul is cancelled because of a typhoon. But they say it will be rescheduled for tomorrow. I'm sure we'll make it in time for the wedding." I force myself to sound cheerier than I feel. "Even if we have to swim."

"The weather is terrible here too. It's typhoon season. All the tunnels are flooding. But the forecast is better for tomorrow and the day after." My soon-to-be daughter-in-law is also making an effort to stay positive. "We'll see you soon."

We board the bus.

"I hope this typhoon isn't some sort of metaphor," I say irritably to John. Lucas and Yena had already had to swim through plenty of stormy waters. Sometimes I had felt as if we were swimming along beside them. I was ready for us all to reach the shore.

***

Shortly after Lucas moved to Korea with Maya, she broke up with him, her ambition apparently outpacing my son's. Not long after, he met Yena through a program which brought people together to practice their English and Korean. They slowly fell in love. For a long time Yena didn't tell her father about Lucas, sure that he wouldn't approve. Finally, she introduced him. Then ensued an extended period during which Yena tried to convince her father to let them marry. He refused, offering a litany of reasons. "He isn't Korean! He has American parents! His Korean is very bad! He doesn't make enough money! He doesn't even have a car! He wants you to move with him to the United States! No, no, no."

This list of objections not proving effective, he tried bribery. He offered to buy Yena a car and expensive jewelry. She remained unmoved.

He took the opposite tack. He would no longer support her, as most Korean parents do before their children marry. She would have to move out of her parents' apartment.

She moved out.

We met Yena when we visited Lucas in Korea three years previously. He hadn't told us much about her, but all of a sudden she appeared at his side while we were having dinner in a restaurant. She emerged like a lovely phantom, wearing a pale pink sweater, her eyes shyly downcast. She was petite, with long black hair and porcelain skin. During the rest of our visit, she accompanied us often, although she hadn't yet told her parents about Lucas. I felt as if the four of us were sneaking around Seoul, with its fifteen million people, hiding from them.

A year later she and Lucas visited us for a month in the United States. Despite her excellent English, she had never travelled to a foreign country other than Thailand. We understood that the tacit purpose of the trip was to see if Yena thought she could adjust to life in the United States. I liked her very much, although I understood there was still much for us to understand about one another. And I didn't want to be too hopeful. Lucas had had many girlfriends, and we had always heard that Koreans were prejudiced against adoptees. Would this bias ultimately sink their relationship?

Back in Korea, Yena called me once to ask what to do about her father's intransigent attitude. "Lucas said I should get advice from you. I think we should just elope because my father will never change his mind. He is too stubborn." And that is where you get your stubbornness, I thought privately, marveling at the determination she had shown in standing by Lucas.

"Just wait a little longer, Yena. Your father just wants what is best for you."

"That is what Lucas thinks too."

I hung up the phone, confident that I had given good advice, pleased and a little surprised that my son had shown faith in my judgment. John and I resumed waiting, the posture we had adopted during Lucas' time in Korea. We had no power to direct whatever outcomes lay ahead.

Finally, Mr. Yoo said yes.

**

My father didn't approve of John when we married. Dad, whose hair style and wardrobe remained entirely the same throughout his life, detested John's shaggy hair, his full beard. He guessed, correctly, that John was one of those young men trying not to fight in the Vietnam War. He was shocked that we lived together before marriage. Dad was from a generation that thought a man should be able to support a family before he married. Case in point: he told my mother that he wanted to wait to get married so he could save money. But she persisted. Dad thought that John might leave me when he finished medical school, after relying on my financial support to put him through.

Over time, John earned Dad's trust. I saw Dad watching him, observing the way he treated me. He saw that John had an engineer's ability to fix things. That he was frugal. That he came from a good family, a farm family.

On his deathbed, Dad told John he loved him. And John said the same to him. Love grows from effort, persistence and patience.

Seven years after his marriage, on his fortieth birthday, Lucas will spend the day at his father–in-law's hospital bedside in Seoul. Using the Korean language, Mr. Yoo will recite the speech he has rehearsed, telling his father-in-law that he will take good care of Yena. I don't know what his father-in-law told him. Mr. Yoo will die ten days later.

***

We arrive in Seoul the next day, just as the Japanese clerk had promised. Lucas and Yena meet us at the airport and we immediately rush to the rented van, off to meet Yena's parents. As we speed through Seoul, few signs of yesterday's torrent remain. The sun is shining.

"What should I call your parents?" I ask Yena. "I don't think I know their names."

"We don't really call them by their names," she answers. "The word for in-law is sa don." I never really find a way to use this term. The Korean attitude toward names bedevils me.

We enter the Yoos' apartment, a high rise overlooking an elegant park. It is spacious and sparsely but smartly furnished, with a black-and-white color scheme, gourmet kitchen, and a Korean scroll on the wall. We are introduced to Yena's father, stepmother, and brother.

"Anyanghakaseyo" (ong-yong-a ka-say-o), I say haltingly, hoping I am not butchering the pronunciation too much. Six syllables to say hello! No wonder Lucas is having trouble conquering this language. As it turns out, pronunciation is the least of my worries, as what I have just said means goodbye, not hello. So much for good impressions.

"I'm so sorry we are late. Because of the typhoon." Yena's father and stepmother look equally uneasy, bowing and talking at once, while Yena translates, struggling to keep track.

"My father says you must have been really pretty when you were young."

I laugh, blushing. Her parents are themselves very attractive. Looking at her father, I immediately know where Yena gets her good looks. Her stepmother is beautifully coiffed and bejeweled and is wearing a stylish pantsuit. She looks sad, though, seldom smiling and retreating into the kitchen often. I surmise that she still has trouble accepting this marriage.

Yena's father plays the host well, showing us around. "Beatles?" he says, reaching down and pulling out the "Abbey Road" album from a stack of records near the stereo.

Yena explains. "My father is a big fan of the Beatles."

"We are too!" John exclaims.

Out of the corner of my eye I watch Lucas, playing with their tiny white shitzu, which he has privately joked is the dumbest dog in the world, unlike our brilliant yellow lab. He teases his soon-to-be brother-in-law. He seems at ease here. I begin to relax.

We exhaust Yena as we talk back and forth, telling about us, our stay in Tokyo, our befuddlement by the typhoon which had delayed us. "I was so worried we would miss the wedding," I confess, tears welling in my eyes. I haven't realized how stressed I am.

Soon we exchange presents. The scotch and makeup that Yena suggested for her parents go over well. Mrs. Yoo even smiles momentarily. Yena's brother tries on a University of Minnesota sweatshirt.

"You go to school here?" he says, his English not quite as fluent as Yena's. Yena plans to enroll at the university once she and Lucas move to Minneapolis. She wants to go to medical school.

We gather on the couch to look at Lucas' baby book. "I want you to see where Lucas grew up. Here are pictures of our house. We live on a lake. And here is our daughter. Clara couldn't come because of her work schedule." I don't add that she doesn't like to travel.

Soon Yena and her stepmother go into the bedroom and emerge with an oblong box.

"The hanbok!" Yena announces.

They have ordered a custom-made hanbok for me to wear to the wedding. Hanboks are the traditional ceremonial dress of the Korean people. I have read they are meant to resemble a butterfly. All stratas of society wear them: if you see a photo of the recent Korean president, Mrs. Park, at a special function, she will undoubtedly be wearing a hanbok.

I open the box, lift the rustling fabric upward. I examine each piece while the two women explain. First I will put on the long white slip. Then a tiny white jacket, also an undergarment. Next, the fuchsia jumper, its full skirt commanding a wide swath of space. And finally a lime green jacket. "Should I try it on?"

"Of course."

We go into the bedroom. After shyly removing my outer clothes, I stand passively as the Korean women, talking a mile a minute, cover me with the four layers of fabric. Will I ever remember the order? Finally, Yena's stepmother artfully ties a little yellow sash which holds the jacket together. I twirl about.

"Don't forget your shoes," Yena says. I slip on pink satin shoes. I don't mention that they are too small and pinch my feet.

"I love it! Kamsamida (kom-som-ee-da)." Trying out another Korean word I have learned. Thank you.

Mrs. Yoo smiles a little and nods approvingly. She brings out another box which contains the hanbok she will wear, in shades of brown and purple. I exclaim some more, making eye contact, wanting to communicate nonverbally that I empathize with her feelings, her fear that she is losing the precious daughter she has helped raise since she was eight years old.

I also want to acknowledge that we have something in common: we are both second mothers. I don't think I succeed.

STEPMOTHERS

Yena and I are both first daughters, first daughters who adore our fathers and have complicated relationships with our second mothers.

Yena told me that once her parents were divorced she didn't want her friends to know she had a stepmother because she was ashamed. Divorces were rare in Korea at the time. She wanted them to think her stepmother was her biological mother. She even told her biological mother she didn't want her to visit. She felt she had to choose between mothers.

I understood. There was a time when I didn't want to admit I had a stepmother either.

In the fifties and sixties I knew no one who had a dead mother. Today Tommy and I would have been packed off to a grief group. But none existed back then. And I knew no one who had a stepmother.

Every-other show on TV seemed to feature motherless children overseen by a widowed and wise father. Stepmothers were nowhere to be found.

I watched *My Three Sons, Bonanza,* and *The Rifleman.* Each show included a house full of males. Their saintly deceased mother was rarely referenced. The men seemed to have such fun with all of that horsing around.

Why no females? I wondered. The underlying message seemed to be that women, especially stepmothers, would just ruin the good times. I think I may have absorbed some of that misogyny.

In books there were also plenty of motherless children. I read *Pippi Longstocking,* but except for our red hair and motherlessness, I couldn't relate. I wasn't that adventurous. I read fairy tales populated with wicked stepmothers. I cringed. I didn't want anyone to feel sorry for me. My stepmother, while not perfect, wasn't wicked.

After my family and I moved to Waterloo when I was ten, I didn't tell anyone that Myra wasn't my real mother. I simply wanted to fit in, doing what other girls were doing. I did my homework, took tap-dancing lessons, joined clubs, and went to potlucks with a small group of girlfriends. I spent hours lying on my bed with the lilac bedspread and matching curtains, despairing over the fact that not a single boy in Waterloo seemed to be aware of my existence, despite the obsessive effort I was devoting to improving my appearance.

But finally, when I was in the ninth grade, I did tell a friend. I'm not sure why. Maybe it was the fact we were babysitting together with no adults nearby, or maybe something had come up on TV, or maybe it was the late hour.

I suddenly said, "Did you know my mother isn't my real mother? My real mother died when David was born."

The world started to spin when I said these strange words. I sunk into a chair, hyperventilating. Pam started to cry.

"How did you stand it? I couldn't live if my mom died?" When we parted, she looked at me with a mixture of pity and awe.

Gradually, as Myra and I grew apart, I told more people. I never asked Myra what it was like to be a stepmother, especially in a time when such mothers were rare. We could have bonded over the fact that she and I both became second mothers. But we never did.

Lucas and Yena, September 4, 2010

24

Jeju Island

September 2010

F ollowing our introduction to Yena's parents, I surprise myself by sleeping well, relieved that we have successfully navigated the first hurtle of this adventure.

The following morning we leave Lucas and Yena's small apartment, on our way to Jeju Island, a destination spot for weddings. Emerging onto Seoul's crowded sidewalks, I thread my arm through Lucas'. As he and Yena expertly weave us through the crowds, I think of the first time we met Lucas at a crowded airport. I trust him now as he once trusted us.

I stare wide-eyed at the hordes of people, their questioning inflection still sounding strange to my American ear. Every-other shop seems to sell cosmetics, reflecting a culture which places a high value on external appearance. Green spots are few and far between. The skyscrapers are crowded together, reaching skyward as if to find a space to breathe.

We reach the airport and load onto a little commuter plane, soon emerging into a different world. When I think of

Jeju, I think of the color orange. Orange signs abound because tangerines are a major export.

"Jeju is supposed to be the Korean version of Hawaii," Yena tells us. "I have always wanted to visit."

The two have purchased a wedding package, which comes with a hotel room, ceremony, reception, and rented wedding attire. After we check in at the hotel, Yena invites me to watch her select her dress.

"Your mother should be here," I say to Yena, as I seat myself in the plush chairs reserved for mothers. I mean Yena's birth mother, who isn't invited to the wedding. When parents divorce in Korea, the father is usually awarded custody. There is no motivation on his part to continue contact with the mother because there is no belief that this is beneficial to children. Apparently years went by with limited contact, although Yena and her mother are back in touch now. But there was no question of her mother coming to the wedding.

Yena has her own version of a missing mother, I think. Maybe that is one reason why she connected with Lucas.

"She is sad not to be here. We will meet her in a few days. But I am glad you can help me." The fashion show begins.

The dresses are typical of Western style wedding dresses, with bare shoulders and layers upon layers of fabric. Yena tries on many dresses, looking like a movie star in every one. Truthfully, they all look good to me, much better than my own wedding dress. I had thrown my simple, street-length dress away a few years ago, embarrassed by its poor craftsmanship.

***

I learned to sew from Myra. I see the two of us bent over the dining room table, patterns and fabric spread this way and that. Although I haven't sewn in years, I am surprised at how viscerally I recall the sewing process: the rustle of the thin paper pattern as I unfold it from its envelope, flattening it onto the chosen fabric. The feel of straight pins attaching paper to fabric, of pulling a pin from my tightly clenched teeth. My tight grip on the scissors as I cut along the dotted lines. I feel the psychological aspect too. Frustration looms large—the frustration of struggling to squeeze armholes into what seem to be inadequate spaces, the tedium of ripping out errant seams. Sometimes Myra took over if I complained loudly enough. But I felt pride, too, when I wore a finished product. I made much of my wardrobe for college and continued to sew most of my clothes while John was in med school.

I made my own wedding dress without the help of my stepmother. And it showed.

**

I say to Yena, "You look beautiful in them all. But I think the strapless dress shows off your skin and shoulders really well."

I don't think Yena is relying on my advice, being a young woman with her own strong opinions, but that is the dress she chooses. She picks out shoes, white satin with towering heels, and then we are finished.

We find the men, who have been exploring the grounds. Later we have a lovely dinner on a deck facing the ocean. We are sharing a newly discovered intimacy with our son and future daughter-in-law.

Lucas tells us how he had picked out Yena's engagement and wedding rings. He bought them from her father, a jeweler.

"I went to his shop and he set in front of me about eight rings. Then he proceeded to tell me what was wrong with all of them except one." He mimics Mr. Yoo, shaking his head and wagging his finger. "Guess which one I chose?"

I don't dare ask him about its cost.

Together, we watch the sun vanish over the China Sea. We go to bed early, dreaming of the wedding to come.

The weather continues to bless the next day. In the late morning I begin to get ready, trying to remember the order of the four layers of my hanbok. I can't figure out how to tie the yellow sash so I go off to find Yena, hating to bother her while she is busy getting ready. But I am unwilling to show up at the wedding chapel partly dressed.

I find her in the hotel's hair salon, sporting enormous rollers on the top of her head while a young woman applies makeup. "I wish my stepmother was here. She knows how to do this better than me. But I think this is how you do it," she says. "Are you going to wear your shoes?"

"Sure! I've got them right here. You better finish getting ready," I say. "We'll be fine. See you at the wedding." I put on the too-tight shoes, which force me to walk with mincing steps. I take some deep breaths and go off to find John.

Walking through the lobby, we are greeted by many smiling, bowing Koreans. A tall strawberry blond in a rustling hanbok can easily garner attention, I discover.

We find the small chapel and seat ourselves in the front row, smiling foolishly at Yena's family on the other side, unable to communicate with them, other than to bow and repeat "annyounhanshimika" over and over.

Except for the specific ocean view, the language, and the bowing that will take place repeatedly, this wedding could have taken place in the US. The music is Western, although I struggle to identify any specific pieces. The aisles are decorated with bunches of pink and white carnations.

Soon it is time to light the candles, the only task assigned to Mrs. Yoo and me. We rise and perform flawlessly. I return my rustling body to John's side, my nervousness mushrooming as Lucas takes his place in front of the altar. He is alone, neither he nor Yena having any attendants. His usually straight hair has been curled. Seeing my son with curlicues atop his head takes some getting used to. But I am more preoccupied by his actions than with his appearance. Will Lucas know what to do, since most of the service will be conducted in Korean?

We stand as Yena enters holding her father's arm. She keeps her gaze demurely lowered throughout their march down the aisle and remains solemn throughout the ceremony. Her father is similarly solemn, while Lucas smiles self-consciously, shifting his weight from one side to another.

The service is generically Christian. Occasionally the minister will speak English and, despite his accent, I can pick out familiar phrases: "the spirit of the Lord," "the holy ghost," "may the grace of the Lord Jesus Christ go with you." Lucas seems to give the correct answers as they are required. He is told he can kiss the bride before the ring ceremony. Chastely, he kisses her on the cheek, perhaps a reflection of Korea's conservative sexual mores.

The couple exchanges rings. The rings are extravagant, especially by my standards, since I have never owned a diamond ring. John and I were poor students when we married and my frugal husband has never thought diamonds a wise investment, even once we could afford it. I agree with him. But here is my son having a ring with its own little diamond slipped on his finger.

At the end of the service, Lucas moves toward his father-in-law. Slowly he falls to his knees, lowers his forehead, then lays the rest of his body before him, prostrating himself on the ground.

I inhale and am still moved when I think of this moment between father- and son-in-law.

We go outside to have champagne. We are given flower petals with which to shower the bride and groom. Yena's father grasps my hand and pleads, with Yena translating, "Take good care of my daughter." Beside him, his wife weeps. In this Confucian, hierarchical culture, we parents of the groom are assuming as much responsibility for Yena's future well-being as is our son.

"Ne, ne," (Yes, yes) we keep repeating, nodding our heads vigorously.

25

Gratitude

September 4, 2010

After the champagne toast, the couple is spirited away by the photographer. There will be a small reception down by the beach later in the afternoon. "I'm going back to the room to change," John announces.

"I'll be there soon."

But as I make my way down the steep steps connecting the chapel and the hotel, decorously lifting the skirts of my hanbok so that I won't trip, a man and woman approach. "Are you Lucas' mother?" the man asks in flawless English. He is tall, wears glasses, and has an earnest smile. The young woman beside him is pregnant.

"I am."

"I am Lucas' boss. This is my wife," he says. We bow. "I just wanted you to know that Lucas is the best teacher I have ever had work for me. He relates to the kids so well."

Stammering, my eyes growing wide, my skin turning

crimson, I thank him. "Were you at the wedding?" I say. "I don't think I saw you."

"We came at the end. We had to fly to get here so we were a little bit late, I'm afraid."

"But you put in a tremendous effort! I am sure Lucas and Yena are very grateful."

"We are happy to be here. We have never been to Jeju Island so we are going to spend time looking around."

We stood for a moment more in the middle of this well-traversed path. I wish I had continued the conversation, but I was so overwhelmed I couldn't gather my thoughts very well. "Well, thank you again, for what you said. It means a lot to me. I will tell Lucas' dad."

We bow again and go our separate ways. But instead of heading to the room, I suddenly veer to the right. After removing my uncomfortable shoes, I walk toward a path parallel to the ocean and find a quiet bench. I sit down, oblivious to the curious glances my formal attire is likely drawing. The generous sun spreads its light across the sea's expanse, shimmering. In the distance, a cloud of birds rises up.

For a while I just watch the breaking movement of the waves, transfixed. Shaking myself out of my reverie, I try to make sense of recent events. I am not sure which is more momentous, my son's marriage or the exchange with Lucas' boss. Both have changed my perception of my son.

The endorsement from his boss, the type of praise that had tended to elude him in Minnesota, has assured me that Lucas is going to be okay—that he has found his niche, that my son is coming into his own. I wonder how much his return to Korea is key to this flowering of ambition and determination. Or was it always present, and I was too blind to see it?

After a few minutes, I look to my right. In the distance I see Lucas and Yena, their movements being choreographed by the photographer. Since I can't hear their voices, it is like a dance without music as they engage in a series of poses: walking along the ocean hand-in-hand, sitting and lying down on the grass, gazing into each other's eyes, exchanging kisses. At one point Lucas lifts Yena into his arms, as if ready to carry her over the proverbial threshold.

Lucas has crossed many thresholds this summer day. He has become a husband. He has been united with a Korean family and is now a bona fide member of their lineage. I suspect his name will soon appear in the family ledger Koreans so carefully maintain over hundreds of years. It is as if he has been returned to a place of belonging in Korea, having been separated from his birth family so long ago to be joined with an American one.

I have crossed a threshold also. Now I am a mother-in-law. I have a new daughter. Yena, despite all of the roadblocks she faced, has not abandoned Lucas.

And I have not lost my son to Korea. He has not had to choose one country and culture over the other. He has figured out a way to belong to both and for John and me to be a part of both. I imagine him reaching toward John and me and drawing us over the threshold that is Korea, making us a part of this family and culture as well. Tying together loose threads.

"You were right all along, Lucas," I whisper. "Things are working out."

I sit some more. I am reluctant to leave this moment, and the ocean, behind. Finally I rise and walk toward the hotel. I need to find John. I need to tell him what Lucas' boss had said. I know it will mean as much to him as it has meant to me.

By travelling to Korea, I thought I was simply going to my son's wedding. But my journey turned out to be bigger than that. I will come home with much more than I left. Behind me I hear the roar of breaking waters.

***

We end the day with a simple reception down by the beach. Lucas and Yena have changed into hanboks. Lucas is clad in a blue jacket and pink pajama-like pants. Yena's hanbok is yellow and red. Now John and I wear civilian clothes.

"I wonder if I can drive a car dressed like this." Lucas jokes.

Although we can't share a language with the other guests, we can share a moment of reverence for our surroundings, for the beauty of the ocean and the orange sun casting its brilliance as it sinks into the horizon. We mingle with Yena's family while nibbling on simple appetizers. I offer a spontaneous toast.

"I know it has been difficult for your family to accept Lucas, but we are grateful for your kindness toward our son and our family. We promise to always take good care of Yena." Yena begins to cry as she struggles to translate. I look around and through my own tears see the tears of her parents, her brother, her aunts and uncles. But they are also smiling and nodding. We are finally sharing a common language despite our barriers.

The typhoon proves to be a sort of metaphor, after all. A framing metaphor. It roars two days before the wedding, loudly announcing its arrival, then drifts out to sea, inviting the sun to take its place. It comes roaring back the day after the wedding.

I find a secluded place in the lobby and stare out the window, mesmerized by the trees I see bending close to the ground, the slivers of rain shooting sideways, the ocean waves attacking the shore. Lucas and Yena join me. John is checking us out of the hotel. We are leaving a day early, due to the weather.

"I guess the sun wanted to be a part of your wedding." I smile. "Now that it's over, it's gone elsewhere."

The valet arrives with the yellow Volkswagon. He offers Lucas the keys, bowing respectfully. I take a last look at my bench as we drive past it, so grateful for yesterday's transformative events.

26

Two More Mothers

September 6, 2010

Two days later, back in Seoul, we meet Yena's mother. She enters their apartment like a whirlwind. She is pretty, with sparkling eyes, full lips, and prominent teeth. Her voice is urgent and expressive. She darts around the apartment, taking charge. She has brought food, a Korean chicken soup. She has brought gifts, a sun hat for me and a billfold for John. And she brings undershirts, tiny stained undershirts which Yena had once worn, preserved over the years. We are supposed to choose one or two. I hold each up to the light, exclaiming how hard it is to decide, but finally choose two. Today, they lie in a cedar chest next to the tiny green and gold hanbok Lucas wore when he first arrived in the US.

Yena tells us a story. When her mother had shown her these same undershirts when they had resumed their relationship a few years ago, Yena had suddenly understood how much her mother loved her.

I know that during the long effort to earn Mr. Yoo's

support for the marriage, Yena had turned to her birth mother, whose name I never learn. This mother was supportive and had wanted to get to know Lucas. Was it because she herself, as a divorced woman, was marginalized by Korean society?

I say, "We brought you a scrapbook so you will know more about Lucas' life in Minnesota."

She and I sit on the couch as I explain the photos. She tells me she has lived with her brother in Tennessee for three years, so she knows a little English. She has been practicing for this occasion.

"What is this?" she asks, pointing to the portrait that the lady at the airport had given us when Lucas first arrived from Korea. I had made copies to include in these scrapbooks for Yena's parents. I tell her the story. She nods solemnly, studying it for a long time. Her eyes fill with tears.

"Would you like to see the wedding?" Lucas asks.

"Ne." (Yes.)

We gather around the flat-screen TV, as scenes of the wedding, featuring Yena looking so resplendent in her wedding gown, float by. Her mother should have been there, should have helped her choose her dress, I think, feeling guilty once again. As the wedding guests, her former in-laws, come into view, her expression turns grim. Everyone is quiet.

We walk to a nearby restaurant for dinner, her arm threaded through mine, the two of us chatting. She tells me that her brother runs a travel agency. She is learning to play the cello. Yena has told me that she lives with a boyfriend, but he is never mentioned.

She has chosen the restaurant. We are relieved to see that we will be sitting in chairs, not on the floor. Restaurants in Korea tend to each specialize in one dish, this one concentrating on pork. She seems pleased that we attack our meals so heartily.

We tell her about the time we visited Korea a few years earlier, when we went off on our own to explore while Lucas taught school. We went into a restaurant and tried to order bulgogi, a dish we assumed every Korean restaurant offered. But the waiter kept shaking his head. He looked at the other customers beseechingly, soliciting their help.

A smiling man came over to our table and drew a little pig on a napkin, complete with curly tail. Finally we understood that the restaurant only served pork. We ordered pork. Everyone laughs.

"You must have encountered lots of experiences like that when you first moved here," I say to Lucas.

"I still do. Only people get mad at me. They think I'm stupid not to have learned how to do things by now." He laughs, his smile giving no clue to whether he feels humiliated by such exchanges.

"Lucas has had to have a lot of courage to live here," Yena says. "I admire him for that."

After dinner, we accompany Yena's mother to a subway. We say our goodbyes, emphasizing over and over that we hope she will visit us in the United States. We want to show her where Lucas grew up. She says that she wants to visit soon. We hug and bow.

As we walk toward Lucas and Yena's apartment, I keep thinking about the exclusion of Yena's mother from the wedding, my heart still breaking for her. Then my mind turns to another mother who is missing. Although he told me he considered doing so, as far as I know Lucas has made no effort to contact his birth mother during his years in Korea. I continue to have mixed feelings about this. Part of me is still enormously curious. Who wouldn't want to know everything they can about their child?

Lucas has always been quite perceptive when it comes to understanding the consequences of one's actions. Whereas reunification with his birth mother might be joyful and enlightening, it could also lead to disappointment, more loss, and unfulfilled expectations. This ability to consider all sides of a decision has been both a blessing and a curse for my son, likely contributing to what I have sometimes viewed as procrastination. So for now she will remain missing.

I can't help but think that she would be so pleased, and surprised, to know that the son she relinquished long ago is walking the streets of Seoul, teaching its children, and married to one of its lovely young women. If she still mourns the loss of her baby son, which I expect she does, it would bring her some happiness.

And if I had a chance to meet this mother, to spend an afternoon, to sit beside her on a couch, what would I say? Or do? I would try to communicate the depth of my gratitude.

I would look at her intently, trying to memorize every feature, noticing her eyes, her ears, her hands, her size, looking for physical similarities between her and my son. I would ask for her life story, about her family, her childhood. I would want to know about Lucas' father. Did they love each other? How was the decision to place Lucas for adoption made? How much did she suffer? Did she regret her decision? Who else knew? Were there repercussions? Are there more children? Has she had a good life? What has it been like to live not knowing what happened to your child?

And finally, I would share with her this message: I hope you don't ever forget your son. Because even if memories of him bring you heartache, he deserves not to be forgotten. Perhaps you have been blessed with other children, but still, never forget this child. He is worth remembering. Because he carries you, and his birth father, within him. The roots of his fine character come from you.

My arm threaded through John's, I look at Yena and Lucas ahead of us as we walk back to their apartment. Speaking quietly, they hold hands, their heads bowed toward one another. I wonder if they are discussing how the evening went: the meeting of a first and second mother.

27

The Ties of Family

January 2012

Removing my hanbok from its oblong box where it has been languishing in my closet, I lift it upward, shaking free its wrinkles. John does the same with his own hanbok, a gift from Lucas' in-laws. John's wardrobe is typically understated, so as he changes from his normal attire into this outfit, with the pink satin pants and ornate lilac jacket, I smile at his transformation. He will do anything to please Yena.

I drop my shiny white slip over my shoulders, add the white undershirt, the red jumper and finally the yellow jacket, leaving the sash untied. I'll get Yena to tie it. I still haven't learned, and besides, I like the moment of intimacy between my daughter-in-law and me when she ties my hanbok for me.

We grab our coats and march out into the winter cold, raising our skirts and pantlegs lest they become soiled by the dingy snow. We drive to the apartment where Lucas and Yena live. A year after their marriage, they moved to Minnesota. They have lived in Minneapolis for six months.

Entering the foyer, we see a hanging scroll which we purchased for Lucas more than twenty years previously, when our family first went to Korea. On the scroll, a stalking tiger moves amidst celadon green bamboo. Koreans believe tigers have protective powers if the image hangs near a doorway. On another wall hangs a framed child's hanbok, the hanbok Yena wore for her one-year birthday celebration, an important milestone in Korea. My cousin Michael framed it for her as a wedding present.

We smell the warm fragrance of the lemongrass in the dumpling soup and gratefully accept the tea our daughter-in-law never fails to offer. We are here to celebrate Korean New Year.

Clara has already arrived. She looks a bit out of place because she doesn't own a hanbok and says she doesn't want one. But she is game to participate in the ritual.

I hug Yena, knowing that she is trying to keep sadness at bay, because she misses her parents and brother. I fear John, Clara, and I are poor substitutes, so ignorant of the customs in which she has participated all of her life.

Soon, the meal is ready. We gather around the dining-room table and begin to lift our chopsticks to our lips. Everyone except me maneuvers effortlessly, while I struggle not to dribble on my hanbok.

After our meal, we prepare for the next step of the ritual. Yena places two wooden ducks on the floor, ducks which symbolize marital happiness. Now our children are going to bow before John and me, asking our advice for the coming year.

As I kneel on the floor, I am enacting the part of a Korean matriarch. A once insecure young woman who wondered if she could parent a Korean infant, thinking she was playacting her readiness for motherhood, is now dressed up in a hanbok, again taking on the role of other mothers.

It's a bit confusing: aren't we also gathered here, in

Minneapolis, precisely because Yena refused to follow her father's advice? He forbade her from marrying Lucas. He certainly didn't advise her to move to Minneapolis. And I know for a fact that he and his wife have been recommending grandchildren without apparent results.

Does Yena feel herself confused as well, as she has begun straddling two worlds, the Korea of her past, the United States of her future?

I look at my daughter. She seems firmly placed within Minnesota, but still suffers reminders of her past when people ask her where she is from or blatantly discriminate against her. She is both the child of upper-middle-class parents and the child of a mother who likely lives in desperate poverty.

Perhaps Lucas has been the most successful in straddling two worlds. He has lived in both cultures and speaks some Korean. He has given back to his birth culture by teaching its children. His children will have Korean faces but a mix of American and Korean values. Maybe he has threaded the needle.

Lucas and Yena bow solemnly. John and I shift to get comfortable. John hands them each an envelope containing money. We have been told this is the custom, but Yena is too polite to tell us how much money is expected. I have joked to John that perhaps if we gave more, we would get grandchildren sooner.

We begin to dispense advice. Be honest. Be kind. Value your friends and family. Take responsibility for the choices you make. Advice that traverses all cultures and families.

Esther Bordwell and Martha

28

A Community of Women

March 2013

I am sitting with my mother-in-law in her living room. Esther is eighty-nine now. Physically she seems frail, her back bent, her steps slow. And although she is occasionally forgetful, she retains an active involvement in the small town where she has lived all of her life.

Of my children's grandparents, she is the best. I have never met a person so willing to set aside adult pursuits to give her full attention to her grandchildren. Because of her selflessness and positive attitude, she is adored by many, especially by her five children. I adore her too.

She is telling me about her writing group which meets this afternoon at the library. Like me, she is a writer. She has had essays published in her hometown newspaper. "Are you going to read something to the group today?" I ask.

"Probably. I'm thinking about reading what I wrote about my best and worst days."

"That sounds interesting," I say, already starting to wonder how this subject applies to my own life.

"Both days involve Rick," She begins. "The best day of my life was the day I gave birth to Rick. He was my parents' first grandchild. My folks were so thrilled."

"That makes sense. And the worst day?"

"When Rick called me from Boston to say his daughter had had a stroke and was in surgery. He could barely speak. I hadn't known him to cry since he was a little boy." Her voice is uncharacteristically solemn.

Rick's daughter had a major stroke when she was twenty-three due to an undiagnosed birth defect. She almost died.

I think about this choice. Esther has had her share of hardships. She was born with cataracts, resulting in a lifetime of impaired vision. Two sisters have died, one very young. She is divorced, partly because her husband developed mental illness in middle age. The divorce was deeply humiliating, the first to occur within her generation of her family. A daughter has had breast cancer. She could have picked any of these troubles. But she chose her granddaughter's stroke.

Esther had mentioned this phone call from Rick before, how much it impacted her. That a grandchild could die! But her despair went further. She couldn't bear to hear Rick's devastation and to be so far away from him, unable to offer much comfort.

***

Later, I keep thinking about our conversation. What would I pick for my best and worst days?

The worst day is easy. The day my mother died. It upended my entire life, leading to a lifetime without her shelter, a lifetime of longing to remember my mother.

My second-worst day might have been the day I woke to realize I wasn't pregnant after all. Another reason to feel separate and alone. At least with my mother's death I could also feel, sometimes, resilient and brave. Nothing about infertility inspired pride.

I am struck by the contrast between me and Esther. Her best day involved the birth of a child. My worst day did also. And my second worst day involved the loss of a potential birth.

What about my happiest day?

I have had many wonderful days in my lifetime. Most of them involve John and many involve my children. But I can't name my wedding day as my happiest, because of my father's anger and the tension and sadness surrounding it. Nor can I name my son's wedding day, because of our unfamiliarity with the customs and because of the language barrier.

I am sad that I can't choose the days my children arrived either. Although I experienced joy when handed each of my children, their adoptions were also saturated with loss, for them, for their birth mothers, for me. As all adoptions are.

***

In the end the day I choose as my happiest does involve my children. In fact, it involves almost everyone.

One year after their marriage, when Lucas and Yena moved back to the United States, John and I planned a reception. The two were still in Korea, so we were mostly on our own as we prepared. We spent the summer polishing and pruning every square inch of our home, indoors and out. And although we had little experience with formal events, we ordered a tent, we had invitations printed, we reserved plates and silverware. We visited bakeries and sampled ice cream and cupcakes. My cousins Michael and Carmen took charge of the floral arrangements. Clara was assigned to serve the desserts.

When the special day arrived, friends from Iowa City and the Twin Cities, neighbors, and relatives converged in our backyard, Crooked Lake hovering in the background. Friends of Lucas from high school and college mingled together.

My mother-in-law oversaw the guest book. Dad, arriving alone due to Myra's frail health, held court as my girlfriends approached one by one, introducing themselves and telling him how much they had heard about him over the years. Yena's parents and brother (but not her birth mom) travelled from South Korea, a daunting adventure for them. It was as if all the threads from our lives converged, knitted together.

During the party, there were many memorable moments. A next-door neighbor sneaked Yena's nervous father and brother over to his house to share an elicit cigar. A Korean woman, the mother of one of Lucas' friends, oversaw the cooking. Mrs. Yang refused to accept a payment, even as I chased her down the driveway with a check in my hand, my speed compromised by my hanbok. At the end of the day, my face ached, because I couldn't stop smiling.

But one ordinary moment stands out more than all of the others. Right before guests were to arrive, I made my way to our bedroom, preparing to get dressed in my hanbok. I invited Esther to come and watch. She seated herself on our bed. My best friend Carol, who I often think of as a sister and who was cohosting the party, and my cousin Carmen followed me, curious to see the hanbok. They oohed and aahed as I donned the layers. When it was time to tie the bow on the jacket, we put out a call to Yena, who went to find her stepmother. Clara wandered in, looking lovely in the black sundress with red shoulder straps purchased the day before.

Yena's stepmother somberly tied the bow, then patted my shoulders and looked into my eyes, finally smiling. There, surrounded by these six women, I felt more joined with other women than I ever had in my life. I was part of a community of women, engaged in a womanly activity within the intimacy of my bedroom.

On that day, and especially in that moment, I didn't think about who wasn't there. I thought about who was. Two mothers, two daughters, two best friends. And I was grateful for this unique moment within this circle of women.

29

The Love Bird Pin

December 2013

M other?" I say. "Mother, are you awake?" Myra is
slumping forward in her recliner. I gently prop her
back up and pull a crochetted afghan up to her shoulders. She
doesn't respond. I go back to my place in the adjacent recliner,
aware of the empty space between us. I reach for her hand and
hold it awkwardly as I lean her way. Finally, I let it drop.

I shift uncomfortably in Dad's recliner. A coil sticking
through the fabric is poking into my bottom. The arms of the
chair are threadbare, as are the arms of Myra's rocker. The
rug beneath my feet is faded. The linoleum counter off to my
left is stained. My parents, despite having plenty of savings,
are both averse to spending money. Looking back at Myra,
I notice her pajama bottoms are held together by safety pins
because she has lost so much weight recently. I bought her a
new pair a year or two ago, which I have never seen her wear.

Across from me is a bookcase, stuffed with Dad's
collection of history books, most of them gifts from us kids,

especially from Tom. And beside the bookcase are some cross-stitched decorations, Myra's handiwork. Dad loves to read, Myra to stitch. Nothing in common, I sigh. Except when it comes to saving money. But somehow, they have made their marriage work for fifty-eight years.

We have just arrived in Waterloo to celebrate my father's ninety-first birthday. My sister, her children, my brother David, and my kids are all here. Tom, who lives in Washington DC, doesn't like to travel. But he will likely call later.

As soon as we arrived at my parents' apartment, Dad said Mother had been failing all week, sleeping most of the time. He was waiting to get John's advice about what to do. I have volunteered to stay behind with Myra while the others proceed with the party down the hall. Dad and John and the rest of the family will discuss the situation.

I look over at Myra again as she continues to sleep. Bored, I walk into their bedroom and begin idly opening drawers, looking for the new pajamas. I find them next to her jewelry box, their tags still on. I shake my head.

I pick up her pink jewelry box and begin to sort through it. I love jewelry, but I see nothing I like, reminded once again of our different tastes.

Suddenly my curiosity is engaged by an index card pinned to a brooch. The brooch features a pair of gold enamel love birds, each with a ruby-red rhinestone eye. On the card Myra has written: "When I first moved to Waterloo I used to watch the soap opera *Love of Life*. I ordered this pin from the program. I never wore it much because I was afraid to lose it. But in 2010 it is fifty years old."

I begin to cry, remembering the summer years ago that we spent watching *Love of Life* together.

I go back to sit down next to Myra. I think about what I should say to her. I don't say anything. I don't have the words. I just watch her sleep while remembering the surgery she had two years previously, which precipitated this decline in her health.

***

I pick up the phone, alarmed to hear my father's voice on the other end. We had just left him in Iowa City the day before, where John and I had gone because Myra was having heart surgery.

"How's Mother doing?" I ask.

Dad's voice starts to break. "I'm afraid," he pauses and takes a breath, "she's not going to make it." For a moment I think of Dad's raw emotion when he told me Jean had died. "She isn't recovering as fast as the doctors said she would. She's still unresponsive, getting oxygen."

"I'll come down tomorrow, Dad."

"You don't have to do that, Martha. You were just here."

"I'll be there by noon. I can take a few days off work."

I spend four anxious days with Dad, retreating with him at night to a cheap motel near the hospital, staring sleeplessly at the ceiling while I listen to him breathe in the adjacent bed. I am absorbing a surprising revelation: my father loves my stepmother. He will be devastated if she dies. Until now, I haven't really understood. I have been preoccupied by how little they have in common. But my parents share an intimacy of which I have not been a part.

After spending the fourth day at Myra's bedside, finally able to believe the doctors and nurses who say she's turned a corner, finally able to hold her hand and see her shake her head weakly when we ask if she is in pain, Dad and I leave the hospital.

"I want to go to a nice restaurant, Dad," I insist. "Let's celebrate a little."

We enter a wine bar. On this Wednesday evening, we are the only customers. I order a glass of Sauvignon Blanc while Dad, a lifelong teetotaller, sticks with water.

I look at my father, the father I have been told I look like for as long as I can remember. His face is scarred by multiple bouts with skin-cancer, his bald scalp particularly afflicted. But below the neck he seems a much younger man, slender, loose-limbed, able to cross a room or rise from a chair quickly.

I pause. I take a sip of my wine. On this night I intend to ask Dad a few questions—about him and Myra.

"Dad, is it true you asked Mother to marry you after only two dates? That's what she always says." I have always wondered how Dad could have remarried less than six months after Jean died. Could I imagine myself married to someone I haven't even met yet six months from now, John having absconded or been felled by disease or an accident? Not a chance.

"I guess so," Dad answers sheepishly. "You see, I was pretty convinced that I was damaged goods after your mother died. I didn't think any woman would want to take on three children. But she didn't see it that way, apparently."

"Why do you think that was?"

"Well, she was twenty-nine. Kinda old-maid territory in those days. And I had a better-than-average job. She said once I was the only guy she ever dated that made enough money that she wouldn't have to work."

Dad continues, "I could see she was a real good woman. Didn't smoke. Always worked hard. And I didn't want to marry someone with other children. I was afraid you and Tommy would be neglected if that was the case." He blushes a little. "And she was real good-looking. Good shape."

"But," Dad says, "I was happier in the eight years I was married to your mother." Our eyes meet. Then we both turn away. I don't ask any more questions. I can't. I just nod, my head lowered.

Dad orders pecan pie for dessert. After taking two bites, he pushes it my way.

"Why did you order it if you weren't hungry?" I say, as I pick up a fork.

"It's your favorite dessert. At least it was when you were a little girl."

I finish the last bite, savoring the silky taste of corn syrup and pecans. "You remembered. Pie therapy. It never fails."

***

In my parents' apartment, I continue to sit silently beside Myra as she sleeps, until Dad and the rest of the family reenter the room. Lucas, Clara, and Yena come forward one by one and gravely bend down to hug Myra. "You take care of yourself, Grandma," Clara says.

My nephew moves forward, holding his curly-haired baby daughter. He bends his skinny frame before Myra's chair. "Grandma," he says, "this is Abby. Your great grandchild." Mother opens her eyes briefly and raises her head. It lolls a bit.

"She's adorable," she whispers slowly, her speech slurred. Then her eyes close again. These are the last words I ever hear her say.

"We agreed we should call an ambulance. Get her to the hospital. I told John her symptoms and he thinks maybe her organs are starting to fail," Dad says.

In three days, Myra dies.

Two weeks later I return to Waterloo to help my sister and Dad dispose of Myra's clothing. When I find the love bird pin, I slip it into a pocket, telling myself I will wear it on her birthday. I don't ever tell anyone else about it. I don't know what to say.

GRIEF

As if in a dream, I imagine myself walking toward the point on Crooked Lake where Ruth and Russell's cabin still stands. It was purchased by their next-door neighbors after Ruth died, two years following Russell's death. On my way, I walk by my old confidant, the Norwegian pine, taller, skinnier, and more bent over than ever. Her life has become a bit of a struggle, as she has had to share the sun with the competing trees. I nod, though I don't stop to chat.

I pass thatchy black raspberry bushes, my mouth watering as I imagine tasting the succulent berries which ripen in July.

As I near the cabin, the yeasty aroma of Ruth's Norwegian rye bread wafts toward me. I peer into the windows and see with amazement the haphazardly stacked pots and pans on the counter which were in the exact same place forty years previous. The neighbors have never really found a new use for the cabin. Startled, I hear the porch door clang open and Ruth round the corner, quick as a lightning bolt, her body bent forward. Russell follows behind her, hands me a tart gin and tonic, and introduces me to newly arrived guests.

Pulling myself away from the cabin, I approach the lake. On this late September morning, the air smells clean, washed by an overnight rain. I marvel at the Van Gogh-like combination of purplish skies and gold reeds outlining the shore. Slowly I walk rightward, toward the swimming beach, now cluttered with the plastic water toys used by our neighbors' kids. Fifty feet from the shore an old wooden raft still sways. I hear the squeals of my children as they struggle up its ladder and jump off its edges. Continuing along the shore, the faces of Lucas and Clara pull me forward, beckoning me to examine the creation they have forged in the sand.

I see myself wading into the water, fearing its cold, craving its warmth, wondering whether to trust my body to these waters. Like a clay statue, I stand immobile in the water, shivering. I will my body to flow with the water, to trust its embrace. To move forward.

Grief is like entering cold waters. Its force can paralyze or propel.

Taking a breath, I bend my knees and submerge my torso. I begin to swim, my spindly arms thrashing. Gaining confidence, I throw caution to the wind, my body made weightless by the water. I oscillate round and round, ending up on my back, where I squint joyfully toward the clouds, the arms of Crooked Lake holding me aloft.

*Clara, Martha, John and Lucas outside
the home on Crooked Lake*

30

Fall

September 2015

I make my way to the circular table situated on a recessed corner of our deck, a spot that has served as my refuge over the years. My children will be arriving soon from their homes in the cities. Until they arrive, I am traveling down Memory Lane.

When I sit in this space, I feel completely alone, despite the dull din of highway traffic in the distance. I am hidden from the neighbors, yet my view is wide. I see pewter-hued Crooked Lake floating in the distance. I gaze up at the trees, arching my neck. Some have been standing for all the years we have lived here, and some were planted when their predecessors succumbed to oak wilt or green ash borers. The new kids on the block, so to speak, are the maples and ironwoods. I used to see phlox and pink coneflowers until ravenous deer got the best of them and of me. Rhododendrons continue to bloom in the spring, a bit gnawed on, but still teeming with frothy pink and white blooms. I don't expect to see them again. We won't be here next spring.

Thinking I hear a car, I rise and walk around the corner. The three kids have arrived together. Lucas unleashes his yellow lab's seatbelt. Who knew dogs have seatbelts? Ari bounds from the car, thrilled to arrive at the lake where she loves to swim and retrieve. Lucas follows his dog like a proud father attending to a toddler.

Yena unloads her contribution to the meal, as does Clara. Clara wears a baggy T-shirt, jeans, and no makeup. Yena is never without makeup and wears a stylish short skirt. Yena smiles broadly and greets me effusively. Clara is more subdued.

Up to now, the kids have seemed stoic about our decision to move. It surprises me. "It's about time" is their attitude, another way in which they display their own personalities and diverge from the excessive sentimentality of their mother. The mother who clings to every thread of connection to her past. But today Clara peers openmouthed into the garage.

"Whoa, what's all this stuff?" she says.

"Dad's packing up his things. It doesn't make a very pretty picture, does it?"

"You guys really are moving!" Clara says. She sounds somber. "It's starting to hit me now. It didn't before."

Lucas says, "I'm a little sad too. I remember there was a time when I thought I might want to buy this place. But it's too far from everything."

"I'm too much of a city girl. He knows I could never live here," Yena chimes in. "You'll love living in the city."

"It will be a new adventure for us."

"Right."

John comes in from the garden, his posture stooped, a consequence of the Parkinson's diagnosis he received recently. In his left hand he carries a battered metal bucket, filled to the brim with peppers, tomatoes, kale, and zucchini. The hardest part of the move for him will be leaving his beloved garden.

"Hi, Dad. Looks like it's a good year for tomatoes," Clara says.

"Yeah, it's been a good year for tomatoes. Enough rain. Not too hot, not too cold. But the weeds are taking over. I'm not putting as much effort into it this year. Kind of sad to think we won't be here next year."

We walk up the stairs we've ascended so many times and enter the kitchen. Lucas says, "It looks different in here too. Where is everything?"

"The stager said we had to put everything away. Especially anything that would, God forbid, suggest a little personality. She told me to put away my Guatemalan rugs and go get something colorful at Target." I like making fun of the stager, projecting my complicated emotions about moving on her.

The kids look over the dining room table, piled high with odds and ends I hope they will want: old photos, tablecloths, an extra iron, craft projects made when they were children. Yena and Lucas pick out a few things, while Clara surprises me by really digging in, filling a large box with objects that she wants. Previously she had shown little interest in these mementos from her childhood.

"I want this tablecloth," she says firmly, holding up the slightly faded red fabric we purchased in Guatemala long ago. I use the cloth at Christmastime because of its color.

"Great, Clara. I'm so glad. And what about these art projects?" I show her a profile of herself she made when in the fourth grade, a perfect likeness. And a vibrantly painted duck she made as a preschooler, which has graced a bathroom for years.

"No, throw them out. But can I have the vases I made?" She took a glass-blowing class in community college, creating two lovely small vases that I like to fill with wildflowers.

"How about if you take one and I take one? You know I love them."

"Let's have the champagne," I suggest. John gets the bottle, and as we all circle him, he pops the cork. I involuntarily duck as it flies through the room.

After filling our glasses, we descend to the deck and sit down at the circular picnic table. The sun sits low in the sky, soft but warm. The yard is ringed with the last yellow cornflowers of the season. Orange zinnias, unpopular with deer, fill flowers boxes. Ari runs down to the channel and immediately jumps into the dark muck of the swamp. She returns with the bottom half of her body blackened by mud.

"It'll dry," I say, remembering the many times her deceased predecessors did the same.

"We have lived here for thirty-nine years, almost to the day," John murmurs, gazing into the distance.

"Maybe we should have moved a long time ago, so you kids would have grown up with more diversity," I venture.

"I'm glad I live in a city now," Clara says. "I fit in better there. But Crooked Lake was a pretty fun place to grow up. We did all that artsy stuff. And I had a lot of friends."

"Here's what I think," Lucas says. "Everyone's life is random. It's not a standard path. I don't think my life would have been better or worse in the city or the country, just different."

"Does that apply to growing up here versus Korea?" I can't help but ask.

"Sure it applies," Lucas answers. "If I had grown up in Korea, that would have seemed best to me. But I didn't. I don't worry about what's over and done with."

"I'm glad I didn't grow up in Guatemala," Clara says. "The poverty. The sexism."

"I agree with you both. There are some places I never would want to live. And I am sure there are others, besides

Crooked Lake, where I would have been just as happy. But I have loved it here. It's been perfect for me."

"Why, Mom?" Clara asks.

"I love the solitude. And watching the seasons change, from the first lacy buds in spring to the layers of green in summer. I have never minded that we can't see the lake in the summer because of all of the trees. Fall is my favorite season because of the colors. But I even like winter, when all the color is drained away and I just see jagged lines etched across the sky."

Clara says, "I liked seeing all of the wild animals and birds: foxes, deer, woodchucks, owls, herons, pheasants. That was cool."

Lucas nods. "Do you remember how we learned to fish off the dock? How we were so excited when we were little kids to catch a three-inch sunny?"

"We were so dumb!" Clara nods.

"You guys had such a different childhood from me. I hardly spent any time out of doors. But I miss Seoul. I guess city life is in my blood," Yena says.

"I liked that I had a big space for a garden," John adds. "And that I didn't have to take down too many trees to find a sunny spot."

"You kept us well fed," I smile, placing my hand on top of John's. "I give your dad credit for figuring out how to situate our house just right, so we would have all that sun pouring in the windows. And such beauty to look at.

"It sounds strange, but when I look at Crooked Lake, I feel like it's wrapping me in a warm cloak." I stare dreamily at the water behind a curtain of trees. "Crooked Lake has protected our family."

Lucas says, "So maybe you shouldn't move if you love it so much."

"I used to think we would never move. But then I

thought, I'll know when it's time. It's time. I'm ready. Ready for a new chapter."

The conversation ends as each of us retreat to our private reminiscences. I resist the urge to keep talking.

I go in to check on dinner. Lucas finds a hose with which to wash Ari, then joins his dad in the garage to survey an assortment of tools and take the ones for which he can find a use. Clara returns to the dining-room table and picks up some photos. She finds a sunny spot on the dining-room floor and lines them up. She is going to take some photos of photos with her cell phone and post them on Facebook.

I turn and stare, momentarily stopping my meal preparations, thinking of the many times in the past when she sat in the same place, her legs splayed, her eyes focused intently on photos glued in a scrapbook. Of the time she announced, pointing to a photo of herself sent by the adoption agency, before we came to get her, "I'm crying because you're not there, Mommy." Explaining to me that I was the missing mother.

Her expression is as grave as it was the first day we met.

*Dad on the porch of the farmhouse
where he grew up, 2015*

31

Fatherless

March 2016

As I near this book's completion, my father unexpectedly, despite his ninety-three years, enters hospice. I become his primary caretaker. For exactly twenty-eight days, I sit beside him. Dad edges closer to death, while I edge closer to acceptance. We don't talk much because I sense that Dad's preparation involves turning inward. We have spent a lot of time together in the past few years, sharing many intimate conversations. It seems enough.

We hold hands. "My hands look like a miniature version of yours, Dad. Two redheads with wrinkled skin." I ask John to take a photo. It is this image of our hands which I hope will comfort me after Dad is gone.

It seems incredible that Dad has lived sixty years longer than my mother did, with no trace of memory loss and an ability to jump up out of a chair like a much younger man. He has buried two wives. Myra died two years ago after a long and slow decline. All of his siblings are gone, Aunt Nancy dying last spring. I delivered a eulogy at her funeral, during which I thanked her for helping out our family when we most needed her.

David, Dad, and Martha outside the house in Cleveland where David lived with Aunt Nancy's family, when we were in Cleveland for Nancy's funeral, 2015

* * *

Since Myra's death, I have visited him once a month in Waterloo, pumping him for stories about his and his forebearers' lives.

A few years ago I decided to write a children's book for family about my paternal grandmother, who died when I was a baby. I have always wished I had known her, because she seemed like such an impressive woman. She was a college graduate (class of 1909) who took over and ran the family farm in Wisconsin. She was adored by all six of her children.

She and I share a middle name. And although I personally can't see much of a resemblance when I look at rare photos, I assume I look like her, since I look like Dad and everyone says he looks like his mother.

Dad provided me with lots of information for the book and was enormously proud of the finished product. But in the course of our conversations about my grandmother, Dad told me a story which surprised me—to say the least.

"After you were born, I had to work six days a week, so we could never get to the farm. But one Saturday in August I had the day free, so on the spur of the moment Jean and I decided to drive from Waterloo to the farm to see my folks and show you off. It was the first trip you ever took, I guess.

"It was a real hot day, in the nineties. We didn't call ahead, because long-distance calls were too expensive back then."

"You mean they hadn't seen me yet?" I asked. I made a mental calculation. "I must have been about nine months old."

"No, they never had. Farm folks were pretty tied down. And Ma never learned to drive. Anyway, we got there a little after noon. I laid on the horn to tell them we were there. Ma came running out to the car and grabbed hold of you right away."

"I bet she was glad to have a baby girl in the family, after five boys."

"That's for damn sure. And you looked just like me, with your bald head. She spent the afternoon holding you and playing with you. I never saw her so happy. You were the first and only grandchild, so far. And I still remember the look on Jean's face, how proud she was.

"Then Ma went and made dinner for us all. But after dinner she said she had an awful headache and went upstairs to lie down in Nancy's bed. When she didn't come down my brother Jim went to check on her. He started yelling.

"We ran upstairs. Ma seemed paralyzed. She had a really scared look on her face that I'll never forget. Dad called the doctor. He came and said she'd had a stroke. The doc said to take her to the hospital. The volunteer rescue squad had to come with a flexible basket to take her down the stairs, since an ordinary stretcher couldn't navigate around the posts. By the time she got to the hospital, she was already dead. Barely sixty-one years old. We knew she had high blood pressure, but still it was a shock. Your mother had to go out and buy a new dress for the funeral, since she hadn't brought a good one with her."

I couldn't believe Dad hadn't told me this before. He shrugged. "You never asked."

When I tell my friends this story, the sardonic ones say, "You killed your grandmother."

The more diplomatic ones say, "I hope you don't feel like you killed your grandmother."

They, like me, don't know whether to laugh or cry. Is this story happy or sad? I lean toward happy. My grandmother and I shared one memorable afternoon together after my very first car trip. And even though she wasn't physically present during the rest of my life, she influenced me, because she influenced Dad. Because he adored his mother, he learned to love and respect other women and to be a good husband to two wives. He learned to be a good father to me.

I imagine my grandmother taking her place in a line of dead mothers. Jean. Myra.

I add to the line my living mother-in-law, the best mother I know. Then comes my imaginary mother, the old-lady Norwegian pine. She is followed by my children's missing birth mothers. I bring up the rear.

***

Fate dictated that Dad be the parent who raised me. I believe he has loved me even more than my mother would have loved me. He has been my cheerleader and protector for almost sixty-seven years.

Now the roles are reversed. Since he wants to die, I encourage him, reminding him that each loss—of the ability to breathe without oxygen, to walk, to get out of bed—is a sign he is nearing the finish line! I feed my abstemious father the prescribed doses of morphine.

At night, I sit on the edge of Dad's bed and bend down to kiss him good night.

"I'm going to miss you," I say over and over. I become a little girl again, the little girl who crawled into bed with him sixty years earlier, only to learn of her mother's death. My tears dampen his pajamas. Grasping me tightly, he says the words I need to hear.

"I love you, Martha. You've been a wonderful daughter." And the most important: "I know you will take care of me."

On the night that Dad dies, John and I are both sleeping in his room, knowing the end is near. At 2:00 a.m., John shakes me awake.

"Martha, wake up. I think your dad is dying. His breathing is starting to slow."

I jump out of bed, run to Dad, lie down beside him, and place my head on his chest. Within a minute or two, he takes a final breath. I kiss him goodbye.

I have never been present at a birth, other than my own.

But I was present at my father's death. I midwifed him across the threshold, setting him free. I watched him float away into the inky black sky.

When my mother died, it was as if she walked out the door all alone. With Dad, I walked him to the door and helped him to open it.

Epilogue

The Thimble

October 2015

My favorite place to sit in my whole house on Crooked Lake, the place I think I will miss the most when we move, is on my Room & Board couch on our three-season porch. Lucas and I painted the room a mustard yellow years ago, a herculean task because of the many windows and soaring ceiling. Not to mention the fact that I changed my mind about the colors twice, insisting I couldn't live with my first-choice blue which, once on the walls, reminded me of a purplish bruise. Lucas' perfectionism paid off, resulting in a paint job much superior to the result I would have attained if left to my own slap-dash tendencies.

From the couch I can admire the ethnic wall hangings and the masks, ceramics, and photos which bring back memories of our travels to both Africa and Latin America. But I like looking out the windows even more. If I look leftward I can see the lake peeking through the trees. And if I look right I see the front yard, so painstakingly landscaped over forty years. I dug up weeds, hauled load after load of woodchips and planted and replanted hostas, phlox and daylilies, to name but a few. Finally I had achieved the look I craved, woodsy yet colorful. It awed me that I was the one who had birthed such beauty.

So it is fitting that I am sitting on the couch, distracted by the last blooms of daylilies and phlox, when I find the thimble.

On this October day, packing up to move, I sit hunched over a mound of paper which I had saved over forty years, willing myself to toss it all into a recycling basket nearby. Old calendars, used wrapping paper, art supplies for school projects which my children hadn't needed for over twenty years, all saved simply because I couldn't bear to be wasteful. Although I often accuse John of being the pack rat in the family, that label obviously applies to me as well.

The paper is easy to get rid of, but the numerous photos shoved into sundry manila envelopes take more consideration. Although I continued to dutifully maintain family scrapbooks, inevitably there was the odd photo that didn't fit the narrative or that was a duplicate. Plus there were the photos sometimes sent by John's parents and mine, which I finally needed to examine and decide which to save.

I dump out photos from a plain envelope, intending to sort and consolidate. But as I move to throw away the envelope I feel a hard bump in one corner. Reaching down into a corner crevice I pull out a shiny metal object.

A thimble.

I know immediately what it is. And my certainty is confirmed when I lift it to eye level and, through the sooty tarnish, read, in tiny letters, *Jean*. It is the sterling silver monogrammed thimble from Tiffany's that Aunt Nancy had given my mother years ago, the thimble she had thanked her for in one of her letters.

I put the thimble on my index finger and rub its small

crevasses while basking in a feeling of wonder: that I have so improbably found such a small object which means so much to me! I sink further and further into the couch. I try to envision where my mother was sitting when she opened the blue Tiffany box. I imagine her lifting it upward, as I had done, and putting it on her own finger.

But after a while questions start to form. Who had put the thimble in the envelope? And why hadn't I known it was there?

After I read about the thimble in one of my mother's letters to Nancy, I asked Dad about it. He looked at me blankly and said he didn't know anything about a thimble. Since Dad, even in old age, had a memory like a steel trap, I assumed it had been lost long ago.

If Dad hadn't put it in the envelope, Myra must have. She had died almost two years previously, so I can't ask her directly. But I am touched by the fact that she somehow shepherded the thimble through our family's multiple moves, from Carbondale to three homes in Waterloo. Maybe she even used it in her own sewing projects. But she had ultimately made sure that I would get it.

But if she meant for me to have it, why didn't she say anything? Such a small thing, so easy to lose. Wouldn't she have been concerned about that?

The tiny thimble seems suddenly to encapsulate all that was true of Myra's and my relationship. There was kindness involved, on both of our parts. But mostly there was distance, an inability to openly address the ghost of my mother that permeated our lives. I was stunned to realize that we had never talked about her together, that she had never told me she was sad for me, that I lost my mother. And I never told her that I understood how hard it must have been for her to step into such a damaged family and to face the constant knowledge that she was being compared to a ghost. We couldn't find the words. When we did, they were more fraught with judgment than with understanding.

When Myra died, I didn't really grieve her death. I was relieved that I would finally have Dad more to myself—such an admission to make!

But on this October afternoon, I wish she was still alive so I could use the thimble as an entrée into a conversation we had never had. I would like to tell her that even though I knew that on many levels she and I were rivals for my Dad's affection, Dad always had her back, always put her first, as he should have. And that even though he may not have loved her when they married, he loved her when she died.

I don't really know what to do with the thimble. My sewing days are behind me. So it sits in my jewelry box, next to other sentimental objects from my past. And when I take it out and polish it, as I did recently, I am struck by the irony. I longed to find the thimble to bring me closer to my mother. But instead, it brought me closer to Myra, It brought me to a new way of thinking about our relationship. And it finally made me sad that she was gone and I hadn't said what I needed to say. I never thanked her.

The thimble will remind me of what I need to say to my son and daughter.

Acknowledgments

The gestation period for *Missing Mothers* was five years. It never could have been birthed without a legion of supporters. I owe a huge debt of gratitude to the following individuals.

My teachers: Rachel Gabriel, my first instructor at the Loft, whose feedback gave me the confidence to think of myself as a writer; David Mura, who suggested I write a memoir about maternal loss after reading an essay I submitted for his class; and, especially, Mary Carroll Moore. After writing a truly terrible first draft, I wised up and enrolled in Mary's series of online classes, *Your Book Starts Here*. Because of her deft combination of nurturing and no-nonsense, I wrote and rewrote my memoir until I had a finished draft. Then I hired Mary as a private coach to help me structure the book into its finished product. I can't thank her enough. I also wish to thank all of my fellow classmates at the Loft who read and reread my work, always kind, but always bursting with ideas to improve the telling of my story. And I extend my appreciation to my first writers' group at the Loft, including Beth Hannan, Jeff Thompson, Maya Hanna, and Jan Laude, who also encouraged me to keep writing when I didn't know where I was headed.

My team: When the book was mostly finished, I solicited

feedback from a group of beta readers—Lucy Fischer, Patricia Cumbie, and Sandra Nicholson—who provided crucial advice while also assuring me that the book was (almost) publication ready. My copy editor, Kathy Coughlin, and proofreader, Mary Auxier, humbled me by finding errors on almost every page, but because of them the book was polished and perfected. Sabra Waldfogel guided me through the pre- and post-publication process and Patti Frazee delivered an interior I love. John Bordwell took the cover photo and many photos within the book. EBook Launch turned John's photo into the cover I imagined.

My friends: My precious friend Carol Stoddart read all of my early efforts, telling me I had a bright writing future even when I had so much to learn. I hope she can see how much I have improved. I made many friends since I started writing, including Judy Liautaud, Patricia Cumbie, Sandra Nicholson, and Meryll Levine Page. All have been generous with their time and with their advice, both about writing and about publishing.

My family: My children, Lucas and Clara, whom I love, value and respect more each day, gave me permission to tell not just my own story but theirs. I have tried not to betray their trust.

Esther Bordwell, the best mother I know, has also been the best mother-in-law any woman could want. Her praise of the book before it was published meant the world to me. I am glad she is here to witness its birth. My parents aren't here, but this book was written, in part, to honor their memory. My father, Richard, guided and protected me for sixty-seven years. My mother, Jean, would have been proud of how he kept our family together after her sudden death. Although I have few memories of her, my mother's early nurturing created the conditions for me to live a joyous and productive life. My stepmother, Myra, bravely stepped into an impossible role. I regret that it is too late to share with her the insights I gained while writing this book.

Finally, I wish to thank my husband, John, the finest man I have ever known. His unwavering love and support has made everything possible.